EVERYTHING!
CHILD PSYCHOLOGY AND ~~WITHDRAWN~~
DEVELOPMENT BOOK

Dear Reader,

I was very pleased when the opportunity came along to write this book about child psychology because I believe all children would be better off if all the adults with whom they came in contact knew more about how children think and how they behave.

Too often, I have found, adults who are raising children and adults who are teaching or otherwise responsible for children, just do not know or have a keen grasp of what to expect of children at various ages and stages. In effect, many parents and caregivers subscribe to myths about children. As long as adults believe in these myths, children and teens will be misunderstood. When children are misunderstood, adults will have unrealistic and inappropriate expectations.

It is for that reason that I have written this book. I want to dispel myths about what to expect of children at various stages. I want you the reader to know what you should expect of children, from the fussiness of infants with difficult temperaments, to the risks that even normal teenagers often take.

The more you know about children and adolescents and the way they think, the more likely you will be able to provide children what they need and the better prepared you will be to help them grow into healthy and mature individuals. Once you understand how children are supposed to think and behave, the better you will become at helping them grow.

James Windell

Welcome to the EVERYTHING® Series!

These handy, accessible books give you all you need to tackle a difficult project, gain a new hobby, comprehend a fascinating topic, prepare for an exam, or even brush up on something you learned back in school but have since forgotten.

You can choose to read an Everything® book from cover to cover or just pick out the information you want from our four useful boxes: e-questions, e-facts, e-alerts, and e-ssentials.

We give you everything you need to know on the subject, but throw in a lot of fun stuff along the way, too.

We now have more than 400 Everything® books in print, spanning such wide-ranging categories as weddings, pregnancy, cooking, music instruction, foreign language, crafts, pets, New Age, and so much more. When you're done reading them all, you can finally say you know Everything®!

QUESTION

Answers to
common questions

FACT

Important snippets
of information

ALERT

Urgent
warnings

ESSENTIAL

Quick
handy tips

PUBLISHER Karen Cooper

MANAGING EDITOR, EVERYTHING® SERIES Lisa Laing

COPY CHIEF Casey Ebert

ASSISTANT PRODUCTION EDITOR Melanie Cordova

ACQUISITIONS EDITOR Brett Palana-Shanahan

SENIOR DEVELOPMENT EDITOR Brett Palana-Shanahan

EDITORIAL ASSISTANT Matthew Kane

EVERYTHING® SERIES COVER DESIGNER Erin Alexander

LAYOUT DESIGNERS Erin Dawson, Michelle Roy Kelly, Elisabeth Lariviere

Visit the entire Everything® series at *www.everything.com*

THE
EVERYTHING®
CHILD PSYCHOLOGY AND DEVELOPMENT BOOK

A comprehensive resource on how children think, learn, and play—from the final months leading up to birth to their adolescent years

James Windell, MA

Avon, Massachusetts

To Jane, the love of my life

An Everything® Series Book.
Everything® and everything.com® are registered trademarks of F+W Media, Inc.

Published by Adams Media, a division of F+W Media, Inc.
57 Littlefield Street, Avon, MA 02322 U.S.A.
www.adamsmedia.com

ISBN 10: 1-4405-2933-7
ISBN 13: 978-1-4405-2933-7
eISBN 10: 1-4405-3336-9
eISBN 13: 978-1-4405-3336-5

Printed in the United States of America.

10 9 8 7 6 5 4 3 2 1

This book is available at quantity discounts for bulk purchases.
For information, please call 1-800-289-0963.

Contents

Acknowledgments

I have many people to thank for their contributions to this book. First and foremost, thank you to my wife Jane, and my friend Dave Cutting, both of whom provided encouragement and support during this project. Also, I'd like to extend my thanks to Laurie Miller for her contributions regarding the brain.

There are many other people who have contributed in one way or another, even though they may not be aware of it. Mostly they are friends and colleagues, such as Mary Seyuin, who have answered questions or given me encouragement. But I also owe so much to so many children and adolescents whom I have seen in therapy and in group treatment over many, many years. They have all helped educate me about how young people think and behave. And, too, I want to offer a special thanks to hundreds of parents who have talked to me and presented me with problems with their children, forcing me to come up with answers and develop theories about why kids act the way they do.

Top 10 Things You Will Learn
from This Book

1. Understanding child psychology and child development will help you be a better parent or caregiver.

2. Developmental milestones are flexible and general guidelines—not rigid and inflexible rules.

3. Mothers should not smoke, abuse alcohol, or use illicit drugs during pregnancy.

4. Establish a strong attachment relationship with your child by being responsive in the first years of life to their needs.

5. Provide emotional, cognitive, and environmental support to help children have higher levels of self-regulation.

6. Prompt, appropriate responses to your baby's signals increase the child's confidence in your accessibility and responsiveness.

7. Handle a toddler or young child's tantrums by ignoring the child's behavior but protecting the child at the same time.

8. You should expect if you are doing a competent job of placing limits on your children that they will occasionally be furious with you.

9. Allow teenagers more freedom and responsibility while being ready to rein in the adolescent if he shows he can't handle the freedom he's been given.

10. Successful parents tend to be firm, consistent, warm, and nurturing to their children.

Introduction

IF MANY PARENTS DO not understand all there is to know about child psychology, they should be comforted by the fact that not even the experts know everything about child psychology. One of the primary reasons for this lack of understanding is that child psychology continues to be an emerging field. There are new discoveries about the development of children every day. Child psychologists and child developmental specialists are using today's sophisticated technology as well as clever experiments to find out how children develop, what they remember, how their brains work, and how they think.

While each stage of childhood brings new cognitive abilities and new behaviors, it is important to understand the overall development of children and the way their development brings about changes and, ultimately, growth. Many of the changes throughout infancy, childhood, and adolescence are not necessarily welcomed by parents. However, even the most distressing behaviors need to be understood in the context of the gradual maturation of children in order that any particular behavior is not judged simply on the basis of what it appears to be. Every behavior of a child—perhaps, indeed, of any person—must be placed within in the context of development. Only then can it truly be understood.

Parents and other adults who work with children need to understand what is behind the behavior of children. The key word is understanding. The more parents and other adults understand about children, the better they can anticipate what's coming, and the more expertise they will have in coping with—or helping children and teens cope with—attitudes, moods, and behaviors. What you may find in this book is that there are many behaviors that are somewhat strange or even bizarre, but that are, nonetheless, quite normal. In studying child psychology, it is important to see that what many children do is one of the best guides for determining what is normal.

This book contains a great many descriptions of behaviors that often cause parents and teachers concern. These behaviors will be explained and parents will be provided with the criteria for deciding whether a behavior or symptom requires professional help, or whether it is something the parents can handle. In addition, there are many useful tips for parents, caregivers, teachers, and other adults who are responsible for guiding and teaching young people. These tips, I hope, will help adults cope successfully with children and teens.

Finally, you should be aware that I have tried to use the most recent evidence available to bring you what is currently known about the psychology and the development of children. From what to expect of the newborn through how to cope with the behavior of teenagers, it's all here. And it's all waiting for you to learn more about how children think and behave.

I hope that, after reading this book, you will end up as excited as I am about the truly amazing way children develop and grow into adult-like adolescents. It's a wonderful journey from conception to the independent teenager. I hope you find that by knowing more about the side trips and rough spots in this journey you will think it worth all the effort to accompany your child or a child you care for. It is a fun trip and the destination—a happy, healthy, successful young adult—is truly rewarding.

CHAPTER 1

Road Maps in Growing Up

Having dreams and goals for a child make the knowledge of child psychology and child development necessary. It is one thing to imagine the fantastic potential a child has. But parents need practical information to take an active part in guiding and encouraging the best possible development of a child, while helping her reach her greatest possible potential. The more parents, teachers, and caregivers know about children, the better prepared they will be to guide a child to develop both a sound mind and stable emotions.

From Tiny Infant to Confident Student

Child psychology and child development offer reliable road maps for the healthy maturation of children. **Child development** has to do with the pattern of change that begins literally at conception and continues through adolescence. By learning more about the pattern of changes in children's lives, parents and caregivers can view childhood as several unique and distinct periods. In each of these periods children must accomplish certain skills and tasks. Child psychology experts refer to these accomplishments as mastering specific tasks or skills that prepare children for later periods of development. By helping children succeed at these tasks, parents and caregivers can help them go from one period to another as they move toward adulthood.

FACT

Although it wasn't always true, these days the distinct stages of childhood are viewed as special times of growth and change. Parents and educators are more likely nowadays to invest resources, time, and energy in caring for and educating children so they can achieve optimal mastery at each period of development.

When infants are born, they are unable to care for themselves. They require nurturing parents and caregivers who will meet their needs. If loving and caring child-care providers can meet most or all of the needs of vulnerable babies and protect them from the many potential risk factors—often referred to as stressors—in their environments, then the babies will grow and mature. They will develop from fragile, dependent infants to intelligent, resilient young adults who have mastered the necessary skills allowing them to be self-confident **adolescents** ready to leave home and take on the rigors and challenges of college life or the world of work.

What Parents and Caregivers Need

For children to reach late adolescence with all the skills they need to leave the comfort of their homes and the safety of life with their parents and begin adulthood, parents and caregivers must have a working knowledge of child psychology. It is not enough to parent a child haphazardly. Parents must be fully prepared for raising and teaching children by learning all they can about how to enhance the healthy development of children.

Not knowing or understanding how children grow, not having realistic expectations for kids, not having a basic knowledge of the tasks children need to master in each stage of development, and not being aware of how to ease the challenges of each distinct phase of development often means that parents, caregivers, and teachers have insufficient abilities for helping and encouraging children.

QUESTION

How much do parents know about child development?
Researchers asked that question in a 2009 public opinion poll of parents of children three years of age and younger. The results demonstrated that the average parent doesn't know very much when it comes to child development. The researchers found that many parents lack a clear understanding of when young children are capable of reaching certain emotional milestones. Parents had a somewhat better understanding of when they might meet cognitive and physical milestones.

The Healthy Development of Children

The healthy development of infants, children, and teens depends on various factors. Some of the major components of healthy development include:

- Childbirth without adverse consequences
- A favorable genetic makeup and positive inherited characteristics
- A temperament that allows for easy parenting
- Affectionate and supportive parenting leading to a strong attachment relationship
- Protection from risk factors

A child who is blessed with these six factors has a very favorable chance of developing in a healthy manner. Throughout this book, parents will see how these aspects of healthy development contribute to a child who has the opportunity of reaching his or her maximum potential.

ESSENTIAL

The value of learning about child psychology and child development is that such knowledge can help parents: be better parents, know what to expect of children, fill in the gaps in their knowledge of children, have realistic expectations of children, and base discipline on knowledge, not just emotion.

When Do Babies Start Learning?

Amazing as it may seem, babies may actually begin learning while still in the womb. Based on the use of various sophisticated research techniques, researchers have found evidence that babies in the womb can learn. For example, using a nipple apparatus with newborns, scientists have shown that an infant will show a preference for the mother's voice. Other studies have demonstrated, again using sucking of nipples during experiments, that babies can indicate a preference for stories they heard their mothers read during pregnancy. This kind of research is important because it reinforces the idea that learning begins to take place before infants are even born. While some companies and parents have overstated the significance of this research—promoting the claims that babies can become geniuses based on being exposed to music, videos, or the spoken word—it seems apparent that even in the womb infants are soaking up their experiences.

The Importance of Socialization

A major goal in the rearing of children is to help them adapt and conform to the rules and values of the family and the society. This process by which children learn to become social is called socialization.

Starting at birth, children must learn to conform to the rules of their culture and accept the dos and don'ts of their society. In other words, parents and other adults help to ensure that the child's standards of behavior, attitudes, skills, and motives are appropriate.

Parents may think of the socialization process as training their child to mind or obey, inculcating a sense of responsibility to the family, or teaching them to be sociable. However, most parents rely on various learning principles to teach their child to accept the word "no," delay their need for immediate gratification, and regulate their emotions. The various learning principles on which parents usually rely involve modeling, reinforcement, reprimand, and punishment to bring about a child who can take his place in social situations with the least amount of friction. Children who cannot regulate their emotions, are unable to control their behavior, or have an inability to follow the rules, particularly by the time they enter school, are said—often with good reason—to be unsocialized.

Attachment

These days many parents are well aware of the importance of a strong bond between them and their child. And many are certainly cognizant of disorders related to **attachment**. In general, though, most parents are unaware of the extent of research on attachment. They should be aware that attachment—the strong emotional bond that forms between a baby and her caregivers—is perhaps the most important component that helps to bring about socialization in children.

Children who have developed a positive attachment to one or both of their parents will presumably wish to maintain the parental affection and approval they receive. Consequently, they may be motivated to adopt the standards of behavior their parents set for them.

Psychological Theories

There are various theories of how children develop, but there is no one "right" theory; all of the important theories contribute something to our thinking about how kids develop and grow. The major theories of development include the psychoanalytic theory, learning theory, and cognitive theory. There are also several sub-theories, such as the societal theory and the epigenetic theory. The epigenetic theory suggests that development has a great deal to do with genes and what children inherit biologically.

Psychoanalytic Theory

One of the first, and perhaps one of the most influential of the theories of development is psychoanalytic theory. Developed by Sigmund Freud, who lived from the middle of the nineteenth century to 1939, the psychoanalytic perspective on child development emphasizes the psychosexual stages of development. Since Freud's theory of how children grow focuses on inborn explanations of development, it is one of the theories based on what children have inherited and how their genetic makeup interacts with the environment.

Because Freud believed that mature sexual functioning would be the end product of a developmental process beginning in infancy, he ended up calling this process the psychosexual stages of development. But what does psychosexual mean and how are children related to a psychosexual theory?

Freud hypothesized that the mouth is the first main source of pleasure and gratification in the early stages of childhood. He said, though, that as the child matures from infancy the source of pleasure also gradually changes from the mouth to the genitals and eventually to sexual relations with others.

FACT

Sigmund Freud's psychosexual stages included the oral stage during the first year of life, proceeding through an anal stage (ages one to three), a phallic stage (ages three to six), a latency stage (ages seven to eleven), and a genital stage (during adolescence). Freud believed that a traumatic event or an unresolved conflict at any of the psychosexual stages might consign an individual to be stuck at that stage, or it might lead to other negative and long-term consequences.

While Freud's psychosexual stages of development theory has been popular and has had a tremendous impact on our understanding of personality development, there is little or no scientific support for Freud's concepts related to development. In general, experts today believe that the nature of the parent-child relationship has more influence on development than any single event or on unresolved conflicts as Freud contended.

Behavioral and Social Learning Theory

Social learning theory, which started out as behaviorism, had a major influence on practices with children throughout much of the twentieth century. Behaviorists believed that directly observable events—usually referred to a stimuli and responses—were the appropriate focus of child study. In general, behaviorism taught that a child's behavior could be increased through as variety of reinforcers and decreased through punishment, such as disapproval or withdrawal of privileges.

Following behaviorism, several kinds of learning theory—often referred to a social learning theory—emerged. Perhaps the most influential of the learning theories was developed by Albert Bandura, who emphasized that modeling, also known as imitation or observational learning, was a powerful source of development.

Cognitive Theory

Developed by Jean Piaget, who lived from 1896 to 1980, cognitive or cognitive-developmental theory did not receive much attention until about 1960. Piaget did not believe that children's learning depended on reinforcers, including rewards from adults. Instead, Piaget theorized that children actively constructed knowledge as they manipulated and explored their world. Piaget believed that children are born with two mental reflexes to adapt to their environment: assimilation and accommodation. Through assimilation infants can incorporate their surroundings into their existing cognitive beliefs. Through accommodation infants can change or alter their beliefs to accept a new idea. For more on cognitive development see Chapter 2.

What Are Developmental Milestones?

Every parent who has wondered whether her child was developing adequately has sought out answers about developmental milestones. These are the expected ages at which children typically achieve certain tasks or experience certain events.

For instance, for more than fifty years, developmental psychologists have known that infants are capable of directed, visually guided reaching—say, of the plastic rings on a mobile—by the age of five months. This skill then gradually improves and at about fifteen months a young child's reach becomes quite accurate. Thus, it is important for parents to have guidelines for normal and expected development.

Milestones Help Determine Normal Development

Pediatricians and parents are very interested in milestones in order to help determine if an infant or a young child is developing normally. Actually, the assessment of infants begins almost immediately after birth. A newborn is usually whisked away from the mother to be weighed, cleaned up, and tested for signs of developmental problems that could require urgent care.

The **Apgar Score** is widely used to assess the health of newborns at one and five minutes after birth. The Apgar Score evaluates an infant's heart rate, respiratory effort, muscle tone, body color, and reflexes. Following that, other scales and tests may be used to further evaluate infants during the first few hours, days, and weeks after birth. These other instruments include the Neonatal Behavioral Assessment Scale (developed by T. Berry Brazelton and used within twenty-four to thirty-six hours after birth) and the Neonatal Intensive Care Unit Network Neurobehavioral Scale, which provides an assessment of the at-risk newborn's behaviors and neurological responses.

These widely used scales have medical purposes, while the developmental milestones, such as the brief milestones of motor development like visually guided reaching given above, are useful to nurses, pediatricians, and caregivers to determine if a child's development is on pace with the typical child's developmental patterns.

Although these milestones and scales can be helpful, if parents and caregivers regard them as rigid or inflexible guidelines, these markers may result in too much anxiety and unnecessary concern. Used as they are intended, as flexible and general guidelines, they can be reassuring and comforting. However, parents and caregivers must understand that there is wide variability in the development of most children and almost every child varies somewhat from the norm in her behavioral, motor, cognitive, or emotional development.

Child Temperament

Understanding the **temperaments** of children helps to explain the differences in children and the unique way individual children have of responding to their environment.

Developmental milestones in motor development, cognitive development, and emotional development all show the commonalities among children. However, there are also individual differences. If parents don't recognize this after their first child is born, they are usually very much in touch with this concept when the second child arrives. It is the individual differences that make every child unique.

One of the differences that can be observed even in the earliest days of a baby's life is related to temperament. Temperament is the individual infant's typical mode of response to her environment. Some typical modes of response include activity level, emotional intensity, and attention span.

QUESTION

Should I be worried if my child has a difficult temperament?
Research suggests that a higher rate of developmental problems appears in later life among children described by their parents as difficult. There may be two reasons for this: one, a less adaptable child will continue to have difficulties coping with the demands of life; and two, a difficult child is more likely to elicit adverse reactions from parents, caregivers, and teachers. These adverse reactions cause the child to suffer psychological damage due to social rejection.

Three Types of Temperament

In the 1980s, Alexander Thomas and Stella Chess proposed a typology of temperament that has been generally accepted. Their typology classifies infants as difficult, easy, or slow-to-warm-up. Subsequent research by other investigators has confirmed the value of this classification system of infants. It's been estimated that about 40 percent of babies fall into the easy category. These **easy** infants are friendly, happy, and adaptable. On the other hand, about 10 percent of babies are **difficult**. These particular babies may eat or sleep irregularly, become upset by new situations, and may show much more fussiness and crying than easy infants.

The third Thomas and Chess category consists of the **slow-to-warm-up** babies. These children typically show a low activity level, respond negatively to new stimuli, but do adapt—however slowly—after repeated contacts with stimuli and situations.

Risk and Resilience

Every child has to face various risk factors in life. Those children who are able to deal successfully with risks are those who are resilient. An important lesson to be learned from research on risk and resilience is that children who are exposed to various risks may still mature into well-adjusted adults who contribute to society and their family in positive ways.

Resilient children are those who have the ability to rebound from the negative factors in their lives in order to be successful. Negative factors may also be referred to as stressors or risk factors.

ALERT

Studies have shown that household chaos is linked to behavior problems as well as poorer **cognition,** and children's decreased ability to regulate themselves. A home that is noisy, crowded, features family instability, lacks routines, and has the TV on all the time is a chaotic home.

For example, researchers Gary Evans and Kimberly English found that poor children are much more likely to face more stressors than are middle-class children. Those stressors identified by Evans and English include family turmoil, separation from parents, exposure to violence, overcrowded living conditions, excessive noise, and poor housing quality.

Some researchers and organizations, such as the Children's Defense Fund, are concerned about the number of children in our society who are "at risk." Young people said to be at risk are those who are extremely vulnerable to the negative consequences of school failure, substance abuse, and early sexuality. Often, at risk youth live in families that, because of economic, health, or social problems, are unable to provide adequate care and discipline to their children.

How Children Become Resilient

All children, however, encounter a variety of risks, some of which may alter their lives dramatically. And risks come in many forms: some are genetic or biological, such as a birth defect or a serious illness. Other risks are demographic, such as family income or membership in a minority group.

But individual children respond to risks in very different ways. Some, as indicated above, exhibit resilience under the most difficult of circumstances. Researchers who have studied resilient individuals have identified three primary types of protective factors that appear to buffer children from the effects of risks and stress. They are:

- Positive individual traits, such as high **intelligence** and high **self-esteem**
- A supportive family environment where, for instance, there are warm parents and an absence of violence or serious discord
- Positive forces outside of the family, such as social agencies and institutions. For example, a favorite teacher might be a significant mentor in a child's life or a religious institution might provide invaluable support to a young person.

One important lesson to be learned from research on risk and resilience is that children who are exposed to various risks may still mature into well-adjusted adults who contribute to both family and their community in positive ways.

CHAPTER 2

The Great Themes in Child Development

This chapter will introduce seven great themes in child development. These themes raise questions—often questions that parents, caregivers, and educators have wondered about. While there are many theories related to these themes, there are few definitive answers. However, child psychologists continue to explore the themes and the issues they reflect, such as the role of nature versus nurture, the question of when children start thinking, and the mystery of how the emotions develop. Important models of child development feature four stages or levels of development. While it is clear that children's growth and development proceeds through stages, it is unclear whether there are really critical stages of development as some theorists may lead us to believe.

Theme One: Nature Versus Nurture

Nature versus nurture is a theme that has been around a long time and has generated considerable debate. The controversy surrounding this theme usually starts with the basic question: Is nature or nurture more important in the growth and development of children? It's a fair question to ask, but it's not a question that readily leads to a definitive, final answer. However, most modern views of child development recognize the importance of both biological and environmental factors. It's clear that whatever genes and inheritance children bring with them into the world, and whatever the events that happen to children after they are born, both categories have an impact on their lives.

Some researchers in child development emphasize the role of heredity and some stress environmental factors. Some even assume a neutral position and say that the focus should be on how genetic factors and environmental factors interact with each other. As you might imagine, this becomes a very complex issue.

There is no final answer about the theme of nature versus nurture, but given what is known about child psychology, the genes a child inherits may establish a range of possible developmental outcomes. Still, the environment may also have an influence on the genes. For example, a child may be born with the potential to function with above average intelligence. However, if that child is born into a poor, uneducated family that is incapable of stimulating a child, he may actually function in the lower range of his potential. But, if he is born in a middle-class family with educated parents who offer a rich and stimulating environment, this child may perform at the upper end of that intellectual range.

Theme Two: Active Versus Passive Children

This theme can be introduced with the question: Do infants and young children passively respond to their environment or do they seek out stimuli and end up influencing their own experiences?

This question is answered differently by different child psychologists. Some child specialists would say that children are molded and shaped by their experiences. In other words, children are more passive in their development. The adherents of learning theory see children as the product of the rewards and punishments they receive following their activities. From this viewpoint, the environment plays a major role in determining what children learn and how they develop.

However, there are other theorists who believe that even young children exert a lot of control over their own development. For example, Jean Piaget, the highly influential Swiss child development pioneer, along with other cognitive theorists, sees children as active and very much involved in solving problems and bringing meaning and structure to their own lives.

As an example of this more active approach to development, children may actively try to figure out the answers to whatever stimulates their curiosity and interest. Take, for instance, the child who may play for hours with the Slinky-like wire and flexible doorstop on the back of a door. By bending it and letting it snap back to its original position, he is seeking answers and at the same time enhancing his own thinking and development.

Theme Three: Learning Versus Maturation

Again, this theme begins with a probing question: Are changes in children's behavior due to biological maturation or to learning? A related question is this: Which has more influence on child development—is it simply growth—or is it active learning that leads to change?

FACT

Maturation refers to both bodily changes and behavior changes brought about by growth of the child and the passage of time. Learning, in the view of some child development specialists, comes about due to experiences rather than the actions of inborn mechanisms.

Early in the twentieth century, some behavioral theorists, such as John Watson, an American child psychologist, believed that almost all actions of children were learned and not inborn. For example, if a child yelled, "I hate you!" at a parent, a behaviorist would contend that this was learned behavior.

And those who took a maturation position would conclude that if a child showed jealousy toward a sibling then that behavior was a result of growth; in other words any child who had attained a certain age was capable of exhibiting jealousy.

Theme Four: Continuity Versus Discontinuity

How does child development proceed? Is it a continuous sequence of events? Or is it a series of abrupt changes and stages?

Some psychologists emphasize **continuity** in the growth of infants and children. These theorists see change as a gradual process brought about by the interplay of learning, practice, and maturation. To these psychologists, ages are arbitrary and behaviors can appear at any time within a range of ages.

But there are other child developmental experts who see things quite differently. These experts view development as a series of stages. And for them, each stage has its unique characteristics and challenges. For these scientists, children move from one stage to another in a sequence that almost never varies. But in this perspective growth is not continuous—rather it is a series of stops and starts. Sigmund Freud and Jean Piaget would be representatives of the **discontinuity** point of view.

Theme Five: Cognitive Development

Cognitive development is a theme that places a special emphasis on how children actively construct their thinking. Child psychologists who are cognitive development advocates focus on how thinking changes in the development of children. There are three basic theories of cognitive development in child psychology. Two are related to developmental psychologists and these first two approaches bear the names of the founders of the theories:

- Piaget
- Vygotsky
- Information processing

Piaget Theory

In the early part of the twentieth century, Jean Piaget observed his own three children as well as other children to attempt to figure out how children think about the world. He developed various processes to explain how children think. He came up with four processes:

1. Schemes
2. Assimilation
3. Organization
4. Equilibration

Jean Piaget also developed these stages of cognitive development and these along with the four processes form **Piaget's theory**:

1. **Sensorimotor stage:** From birth to age two, Piaget said that infants gain knowledge of the world from their physical activities.
2. **Preoperational stage:** From age two to about seven, the child begins to use mental representations to understand the world.
3. **Concrete operational stage:** From about age seven to eleven, the child can reason logically about concrete events. They can also understand the concept of conservation—that altering an object's appearance doesn't basically change its essential properties.
4. **Formal operational stage:** From ages eleven to adulthood, the adolescent reasons in a more abstract, idealistic, and logical way.

ESSENTIAL

Recent research indicates that babies develop the ability to understand how the world works. At three or four months of age, infants develop expectations about future events. And one researcher has found that by four months of age babies do expect objects to be solid and continuous. That is, babies can understand that one object cannot pass through another and that objects continue to exist even when hidden.

Piaget's Influence

Piaget's observations and theories have had a great influence on child psychologists and developmental scientists. However, in more recent years, many researchers have concluded that Piaget was not specific enough about how infants learn about their world and that young children, especially infants, are more competent than Piaget thought.

Vygotsky and Cognitive Development

Lev Vygotsky was a Russian developmental psychologist who came up with a somewhat different theory of cognitive development. Vygotsky emphasized that children actively construct their knowledge and understanding of the world. He believed that children are much more social than Piaget reasoned, and said that children develop their ways of thinking and understanding things based on their social interactions. Kids develop thinking tools provided by society and their minds are shaped by the cultural context in which they live.

FACT

Vygotsky came up with the concept of the zone of proximal development. The zone of proximal development refers to a task that is too difficult for the child to master without help but that can be learned with the assistance of adults or more skilled children. Vygotsky saw children as learning by interacting with more experienced adults and **peers.** These other people help a child learn beyond the "zone" in which he would be able to perform without assistance.

Scaffolding

In the learning process, Vygotsky also emphasized the importance of **scaffolding**. Scaffolding has to do with changing the level of support. It means than when being helped to learn by someone older or more skilled, that the other person adjusts the amount of guidance to fit the child's current performance. Dialogue, Vygotsky said, was an important part of scaffolding. That included internal dialogue and self-talk as well.

Children Use Private Speech to Solve Problems

Children, according to Vygotsky's theory, use speech not just for social communication, but also to solve problems and accomplish tasks. Very young children use language to plan, guide, and motivate their own behaviors. This use of language for self-regulation is called private speech. Vygotsky said kids use private speech throughout early childhood, and that children who used a lot of private speech are more socially competent than those who don't use it much or at all.

In terms of cognitive development, Vygotsky theorized that language and thought develop independently of each other, but as the child grows older the two things—language and thought—merge.

The Information Processing Approach

The information processing approach to cognitive development is an approach that focuses on the way children process information about the world. This approach is more interested in how children manipulate information, how they monitor information, and how they develop strategies to deal with information.

Child psychologists who use the information processing approach don't typically describe children as being in one stage of development or another. Instead, they describe and analyze the speed of processing information, memory, attention, and metacognition changes over time.

ESSENTIAL

When trying to discover at what level infants think, many researchers have focused on the idea of concept formation. Concepts are ideas about what categories represent. Researchers have found that infants as young as three months can group together objects with similar appearances. For example, conducting experiments with photos of cats and dogs, scientists are able to determine that babies around three months of age can group cats with cats and dogs with dogs.

Contemporary researchers have provided considerable evidence that the speed with which tasks are completed improves dramatically throughout the childhood years. So, instead of seeing development as a series of stages that are distinct, psychologists who favor an information processing approach see individuals as developing a gradually increasing capacity to process information, which allows children to acquire increasingly complex knowledge and skills.

Theme Six: Psychosocial Development

Erik Erickson, a Dane who came to the United States in 1933, was a psychoanalyst who moved away from Freud's theories of child development. Erikson did not agree with Freud that personality is primarily established by ages five or six. Erikson believed that personality continues to develop over the entire life span. His major contribution to child psychology is in terms of his theory of psychosocial development—the development of the person within a social context.

He came up with eight stages of development with each stage posing a unique developmental task and simultaneously confronting the individual with a crisis. The person developed a healthy personality by mastering life's inner and outer dangers or crises, or, as Erikson called them, life's opportunities.

Erikson's stages are:

- Trust versus mistrust
- Autonomy versus shame and doubt
- Initiative versus guilt
- Industry versus inferiority
- Intimacy versus isolation
- Identity versus identity confusion
- Generativity versus stagnation
- Integrity versus despair

Each Stage Features a Challenge

Each of Erikson's stages has a challenge—or opportunity—along with a preferred outcome:

1. **Trust versus mistrust:** This stage lasts from birth to about age one with the challenge being whether the child can learn to trust himself or others. The preferred outcome is that a child will trust himself, his parents, and the world.

2. **Autonomy versus shame and doubt:** This stage lasts from ages one to about three. The challenge is for the child to be able to assert her will. The preferred outcome is that she gains greater self-control without suffering low self-esteem.

3. **Initiative versus guilt:** This stage goes from ages three to about five. The opportunity is that children are allowed to indulge their curiosity and begin to explore and manipulate objects. The preferred outcome is that they learn to acquire direction and purpose in their activities.

4. **Industry versus inferiority:** This stage goes from age five to about age twelve. The challenge is for children to explore and figure out how things work and acquire intellectual skills. The preferred outcome is that they gain a sense of mastery and competence.

5. **Intimacy versus isolation:** This stage lasts from age twelve into early adulthood. The opportunity is for young people to reach out and make connections with others. The preferred outcome is that the young adult will work toward a career and become intimate with someone.

The final three stages are not relevant to this book and will not be covered.

FACT

In Erikson's model, if trust is established early on in the first stage, the adolescent individual will be able to view the world as a good and pleasant place to live. If an individual is able to resolve each stage in Erikson's schema successfully, then he will continue to develop in a healthy manner.

It should be said that Erik Erikson's approach to development is optimistic and positive. His stages emphasize the infant's, the child's, and the teenager's relationship to the family and the culture. Thus, it is a view of development that is social, and outward directed—not an inward, purely internal-looking theory.

Theme Seven: Emotional Development

Emotional development is a theme that runs through the work of both Erikson and Vygotsky. Like other child psychologists, Vygotsky and Erikson realized that even newborns are innately predisposed to sociability. Babies, as can be easily observed, are capable in the very first month of life of experiencing their own "spirited emotions" and of responding to the words, feelings, and actions of others.

As a theme in child psychology, emotional development has to do with how young infants begin to perceive, understand, and respond to their surroundings. An infant's emotions contribute to social interactions. That's why a baby's cries, frowns, grimaces, and smiles are such significant signs early in life.

What Are the First Emotions for a Baby?

The first emotion that can be detected in newborns is distress—usually signaled by cries of hunger or pain. But sadness, or at least sensitivity to sadness, is also apparent early in life. For instance, in an experiment with infants between one and three months of age, their mothers were asked to look sad and appear downcast. The babies responded by crying and becoming fussy.

ALERT

Babies become much more fearful as they mature with a peak between nine and fifteen months. Stranger wariness or fear of strangers is first noted at about six months of age and is full blown at about ten to fourteen months. Separation anxiety emerges at about eight or nine months, peaks at around fourteen or fifteen months, and then gradually subsides.

Pleasure is an emotion that also appears early in life. It is common for babies to smile after they have eaten or when sleeping. The social smile, a smile in response to a familiar face or someone else's smile is seen at about six weeks of age. Full smiles—with open mouth and raised cheeks—are easy to elicit by moms and dads at about five months.

Infant emotions become more differentiated and distinct between the ages of six and nine months. For example, anger may appear as early as four months, but is frequently detected after six months when things are not going quite the way the baby would like. The developmental change in emotions is most evident with fear and anxiety.

What Are Emotions?

John Santrock, a professor of psychology at the University of Texas at Dallas and the author of the text *Child Development*, defines emotions as feelings or affect that occurs when people are in a state or an interaction that is important to them, especially ones that influence their well-being.

As child development experts focus more on the emotional competence of infants and young children, it is important to know what emotional competence means. Emotional competence tends to focus on the adaptive nature of emotional experience. Some child development specialists argue that becoming emotionally competent involves developing a number of skills in social contexts. As children acquire more emotional skills, they are more likely to manage their emotions effectively in various situations. And they become resilient in the face of stressful circumstances. With increasing social competence comes more positive and rewarding relationships with others.

Emotional Regulation

As part of the theme of emotional development, emotional regulation has assumed greater importance in the understanding of babies and young children. During the first twelve months of life, the infant gradually develops an ability to inhibit or minimize the intensity and duration of her emotional reactions.

At first babies mainly depend on their parents or caregivers to help them soothe their emotions. Caregivers may do this by holding, rocking, gently stroking, or singing to the baby. Research finds that the caregiver's actions influence the infant's neurobiological regulation of emotions. By helping to soothe the baby, the caregiver is helping infants to modulate their emotions. In the second year of life, toddlers sometimes redirect their attention or distract themselves in order to reduce their emotional agitation. And by two years of age, toddlers often use language to defuse their feelings and the situation that is upsetting them. If they can't do this, we say that they have a poor or limited ability to regulate their emotions.

ESSENTIAL

Self-regulation refers to being able to control and plan emotions, cognitions, and behaviors. In general, children with good self-regulation are more likely to be ready for school, they are more likely to come to school physically healthy, they are more likely to have a good attitude toward learning, and they are more likely to display age-appropriate social and emotional functioning.

Success in Self-Regulation

Success in self-regulation comes about because of two basic factors—genetics and parenting. Some children are born with traits that are likely to help them have higher levels of self-regulation. But parents have a role to play, too. Parents can provide:

- Emotional support by giving meaningful praise to their child, being sensitive to her needs, and being encouraging
- Cognitive support by offering intellectual stimulation and intellectual resources in the home
- Environmental support that comes from a home environment featuring structure and consistent rules

Emotion Coaching

Recent research has also pointed to the importance of being either an emotion-coaching parent or an emotion-dismissing parent, according to John Gottman. Based on his research, Gottman finds that emotion-coaching parents monitor their children's emotions, view their children's negative emotions as opportunities for teaching, assist them in labeling emotions, and coach them in how to deal effectively with emotions. On the other hand,

Gottman points out that emotion-dismissing parents tend to see their role as denying, ignoring, or changing the negative emotions of their children. Research by Gottman and others finds that children of emotion-coaching parents are better at soothing themselves when they get upset, are more effective in regulating their negative emotions and moods, and have fewer behavior problems than children of emotion-dismissing parents. Recent research suggests that children with emotion-dismissing parents have poorer abilities to regulate their emotions.

Critical Periods in the Lives of Children

For purposes of organization and understanding, child development is commonly broken into periods or stages that correspond to approximate age ranges. For example, the following stages of development are most frequently used:

1. Prenatal period
2. Infancy
3. Early childhood
4. Middle and late childhood
5. Adolescence

These stages or periods of growth and development may be convenient ways of discussing phases of childhood. But are they critical stages? That depends on one's point of view. The most important stages in child psychology are the psychosexual stages of Sigmund Freud, the psychosocial stages of Erik Erikson, the stages of cognitive development of Jean Piaget, as well as the stages of Lev Vygotsky.

However, whether any of these stages are *critical* may depend more on whether one strongly believes in the stages promoted by each of the theorists. Otherwise, the idea that certain stages are critical is open to question. Each theorist may say that one or more stages in his model is critical. That is, they may argue that a child must successfully negotiate a particular stage in order to be ready to take on the next stage or level of development.

Since this chapter has introduced seven themes of child psychology and indicated that these themes raise debate and controversy, the same may be true of critical stages. There is no research that conclusively shows that if a child fails to master the skills or tasks of one level, they will be stuck at that level or be unable to successfully get through a future phase.

Parents and caregivers should keep in mind the conventional stages given above. They are easier to remember than the four different models proposed by Freud, Erikson, Piaget, and Vygotsky, and these conventional stages of development conform to a logical division of the periods of development:

- **Prenatal period:** This stage of development lasts from conception to birth. In it a fetus goes from a single cell to an organism with a brain and a developing body.
- **Infancy:** This stage goes from birth to anywhere from one year of age to as long as eighteen months of age. The most important task of infancy is to develop trust in oneself and in others.
- **Early childhood:** This stage goes from the end of infancy to about ages five or six. Children should master self-regulation and become more independent and self-sufficient.
- **Middle and late childhood:** This stage lasts from about six years of age and goes to about eleven years. Children during this phase should master the fundamental educational skills and learn to form relationships with other children.
- **Adolescence:** This stage goes from about age eleven to nineteen years or later. Teens should become more independent, figure out their identities, and gain self-esteem.

CHAPTER 3

Prenatal Development

The very first step in the development of a human being is the moment when conception takes place. That moment involves a miraculous event when a single cell from a male pierces the wall of an ovum from a female. From that single, unique event may come—nine months or about 280 days later—a baby so well developed that she can breathe on her own outside the mother's body. However, more than half of the time the embryo that results from conception does not survive pregnancy. And a small percent of those that do survive have serious birth defects. Child psychology and child development starts with a discussion of prenatal development and the risk factors that may prevent an embryo or a fetus from becoming a healthy full-term infant.

The Stages of Prenatal Development

Prenatal development takes place in the womb of the mother over a span of forty weeks. Physicians and scientists usually divide a pregnancy, or gestation, into three periods: the ovum phase, the embryo phase, and the fetus phase.

The ovum stage of development lasts about one week and the original single cell, during this phase of development, becomes a mass of about 150 cells that attaches itself or is implanted to the wall of the uterus. At the end of this stage, the second major phase of development, the **embryonic** stage, begins. It lasts from the end of week one until about two months into the pregnancy.

During this second stage there is rapid cell division and differentiation of sex takes place. Also, the umbilical cord forms, providing nutrition and oxygen to the embryo while at the same time filtering out many of the disease organisms and other substances that may be in the mother's blood. The mother's bloodstream opens into the placenta and blood passes through several membranes and allows oxygen and vitamins to pass through. The membranes prevent many, if not all, harmful substances, such as viruses, from flowing into the embryo. However, some drugs do pass from the mother into the embryo.

ESSENTIAL

According to the National Association for Perinatal Addiction Research and Education approximately 375,000 newborns face serious health problems due to their mother's prenatal drug use. In addition to health problems the effects of prenatal substance abuse can cause long-lasting learning and behavioral issues for these children.

Growth of the embryo during this second stage of development is extremely swift. By eight weeks of gestation, the embryo grows to about one and a half inches in length, has eyes, the beginnings of ears, a mouth that can open and close, a nose, hands, and feet. There is also a tiny heart that beats as well as some kidney function.

The third stage of development is the **fetal** period. This phase lasts from about eight weeks until birth. At the start of this stage, the developing organism is referred to as the fetus. Throughout the last seven months of the pregnancy, the fetal stage, the growth and development of the fetus is simply a refining of what has already been started.

The major milestones of fetal development are:

- **Twelve weeks:** The sex of the child can be determined; the muscles are developing; the feet have toes; the hands have fingers.
- **Sixteen weeks:** The first fetal movement is usually felt by the mother; the bones begin to develop; the ears are fairly complete.
- **Twenty weeks:** The hair begins to grow; the child is beginning to look more human; thumb sucking may be seen.
- **Twenty-four weeks:** The eyes are completely formed; fingernails and taste buds are formed; the infant is capable of breathing if born prematurely.
- **Twenty-eight weeks:** The nervous system, blood, and breathing systems are all well enough developed to support life.
- **Twenty-nine to forty weeks:** The nervous system develops further; general "finishing" of body systems take place.

Prenatal development can be seen as regular and predictable. If the embryo has survived the early, risky period of gestation, then the rest of development usually proceeds smoothly. The effect of any outside influence, that is, outside the embryo or fetus, depends heavily on the timing of any intervention or interference. There are critical periods during both the embryonic and the fetal stages.

The Prenatal Environment

The developing organism, early on in the pregnancy, is encased in the placenta. The placenta then becomes attached to the wall of the uterus. And there it remains until shortly before birth. In this environment, the mother's body, and that part of the body usually referred to as the womb, provides a protective and supportive environment that is ideal for the growth of the fetus.

This uterine environment is supportive in that the mother's digestive system and her heart are sources of noise. The mother, who will move around by walking, doing chores, or even exercising, provides a source of stimulation for the fetus.

But even within this protective environment the fetus can be influenced by aspects of the environment outside of the mother's body. While the mother's diet and her emotions can affect the growing fetus, outside of the mother's body the fetus can be affected by such external factors as injury to the mother or accidents.

It is important that parents understand the influence of the internal and external environment. By understanding the potential influences parents not only understand the possible dangers to the fetus, but have a greater understanding of the influences and risks and may take preventive action.

ALERT

There are four major inherited diseases that may affect the fetus and the future child-to-be. These diseases are: **phenylketonuria (PKU)**, a metabolic disease; Tay-Sachs disease, a fatal degenerative disease of the neural system; sickle cell anemia, a sometimes fatal blood disease causing an increased susceptibility to infection; and cystic fibrosis, a fatal disease involving the lungs and intestinal tract.

Maternal Characteristics Affecting Prenatal Development

There are several factors that are related to characteristics of the mother that often result in birth defects. These factors include the following:

- The age of the mother
- The diet and nutrition of the mother
- The emotional state of the mother
- The use of tobacco by the mother
- The use of alcohol by the mother
- The use of drugs by the mother

A woman's body is best suited for pregnancy between the ages of twenty and thirty-five. When a mother conceives prior to age thirty-five, she avoids many complications, including the increased likelihood of her baby having

Down syndrome. In addition, other risk factors that increase after age thirty-five are complications related to labor and delivery, **low birth weight**, and other birth defects. Mothers over the age of thirty-five pose a risk to a fetus. But teen mothers tend to encounter greater risks to their health and the health of their infants.

However, the diet of the mother—no matter what the mother's age is—is also an important factor in prenatal development. Malnourishment can lead to a miscarriage or a stillbirth. In addition, poor nutrition can bring about a premature birth, low birth weight, physical and mental defects, and low cognition in newborns.

FACT

During the course of prenatal development, many factors may result in developmental deviations in the fetus. These factors are called teratogens. Teratogens encompass a wide variety of agents including the age of the mother, her diet, her emotional state, any illnesses, use of prescription and illicit drugs and medications, tobacco, alcohol, and environmental toxins, such as pollution. Teratogens are essentially environmental; however, genetic factors within the mother or child will affect the response of each to any particular teratogenic agent.

Likewise, the emotional state of the mother can play a significant role in the healthy development of the fetus. For example, mothers who are stressed may have troubled pregnancies, miscarriages, long labor, and delivery complications. And the babies they deliver may be hyperactive and irritable or experience eating and sleep problems.

Smoking during pregnancy can have an effect on a fetus. Researchers have found that smoking is associated with problems in placental functioning and with changes in maternal physiology that lead to oxygen deprivation in the fetus and may produce unwelcome changes in the brain of the fetus.

Various kinds of drug use can lead to negative effects on the fetus. Mothers who are addicted to heroin or morphine may deliver babies who are also addicted or who sustain toxic effects from the drugs. Mothers who are heavy drinkers of alcohol or who are alcoholic are in danger of producing an infant who is afflicted with **fetal alcohol syndrome**. Research suggests that about 6 percent of children born of alcoholic mothers have a form of fetal alcohol syndrome. These infants have a high incidence of facial, heart, and limb defects. Such children tend to be about 20 percent shorter than the average child and are often mentally retarded.

The First Trimester

Dividing the prenatal period into trimesters (of about twelve weeks for each trimester) is another system of looking at prenatal development and talking about critical periods of development. Because the **germinal** (roughly the first two weeks after conception), embryonic, and fetal stages are of unequal length, there is an overlap with the trimester system. The first trimester includes the germinal period and all of the embryonic period.

During the first trimester there is a marked increase in the complexity of the organism that is associated with a change in the level of fetal adversity. At twelve weeks of age, the fetus' head is still dominant in size, and by this time males and females are distinguishable from each other. Blood begins to form in the bone marrow, and the fetus is capable of reflex responses when being touched.

The most serious damage from teratogens is likely to occur in the first eight weeks after conception. However, significant damage to many vital parts of the body can occur in the last months of pregnancy as well.

The Realities of the Risks

The likelihood of an embryo and later a fetus developing in a healthy manner is not a sure thing. The fact is that an estimated 14 to 18 percent of all pregnancies end in a miscarriage. One-third of all women experience a miscarriage at some time in their reproductive years, even though they may never actually know they have miscarried.

Some research shows that mothers are likely to experience guilt after they miscarry. A woman may view a miscarriage as a personal loss or even, at times, she may see a miscarriage as a form of punishment for her habits, practices, or ambitions. However, despite what mothers and fathers may feel after a miscarriage, studies indicate that 25 percent of miscarriages are the product of chromosomal and gene abnormalities. The other 75 percent result from problems associated with the prenatal environment. Nonetheless, mothers and fathers too, can feel not only a sense of loss, but both may feel responsible for the miscarriage. That is why both mothers and fathers are in need of social and family support after a miscarriage.

ESSENTIAL

The reason a woman may not be aware of a miscarriage is because approximately 75 percent of miscarriages occur before twelve weeks of development. Miscarriages frequently are both unpredicted and inexplicable.

The Second Trimester

It is in the first trimester that much development of the essential parts of the body begins. But the development of body parts continues into the second trimester. The nervous system, for instance, continues developing from twelve to sixteen weeks. During the second trimester, weeks thirteen to twenty-four, parents can listen to their baby's heartbeat with a special device called a Doppler. An ultrasound or other screening test may be done, which shows the continuing development of the baby. By viewing an ultrasound, parents can figure out the sex of their baby. Risk factors decrease during the second trimester.

The Third Trimester

The critical difference between the fragile preterm baby and the robust full-term newborn is maturation, particularly of the respiratory and cardiovascular systems. This maturation occurs mostly during the last three months of pregnancy in the period referred to as the third trimester. It is during the third trimester that the lungs begin to expand and contract. This process exercises the muscles that are involved in breathing. There is no air for the fetus to breathe, but the fetus takes in fluid through the mouth and nose and then, in a breathing-like process, expels the fluid. In the last ten weeks of the prenatal period, the fetus gains more than four and a half pounds or as much as half of its final weight. The average newborn will weigh about seven and a half pounds. If the fetus has avoided the major risks so far, they are not likely to develop during the final third of pregnancy.

However, fetuses that are not gaining enough weight are at risk of being born with low birth weight. Low birth weight is defined by the World Health Organization as weight of less than five-and-a-half pounds (2,500 grams) at birth. Very low birth weight is defined as a baby weighing less than three pounds; extremely low birth weight is less than two pounds. Infants born weighing less than five-and-a-half pounds are at risk for many problems before, during, and immediately after birth. These problems can affect them throughout life, but the impact of low birth weight depends on many factors.

Birth

When a normal birth takes place, the baby's position is headfirst. The mother's cervix dilates to allow passage of the baby's head. As the birth process continues, the infant's head moves into the birth canal, the vagina. In the final stages, the baby's head moves toward the opening of the vagina. As the head emerges, the head is turned by the medical team and the rest of the baby's body comes through the vagina.

ESSENTIAL

If a vaginal delivery would put either the mother's or the baby's health in danger, the baby may be removed from the mother by caesarean section (also known as a C-section). This occurs in about 25 percent of the births in the United States and involves removing the fetus from the uterus through the mother's abdomen by cutting open the abdomen.

When both the mother and the fetus are healthy and the baby is full term, the birth process can be simple and quick. The newborn starts breathing and crying on her own. As the first spontaneous cries occur, the infant's circulatory system begins to function. Oxygen begins to flow throughout the newborn's system and that helps the baby's color to change from a bluish hue to pink. The infant's eyes open wide and the tiny fingers grab at anything they can. The umbilical cord is cut to detach the baby from the placenta. The infant is wiped dry of fluid and blood, weighed, and wrapped to preserve her body heat.

But then there must be more formal assessment of how well the baby is functioning. One common means of assessing the newborn's condition is a measure called the Apgar Score. From a brief examination, the examiner assigns a score of zero, one, or two to the heart rate, breathing, muscle tone, color, and reflexes at one minute after birth and again at five minutes following birth. A low Apgar Score at one minute is a warning, although typically newborns quickly improve in the first five minutes. If the five-minute total score is seven or better, there is no danger. But if the Apgar Score is below seven, the infant needs help establishing normal breathing. If the score is below four, the baby is judged to be in critical condition and needs immediate medical attention. That's when babies are usually rushed to the neonatal intensive care unit.

Complications of High-Risk Babies

For high-risk infants who survive, complications may await. These complications may include medical problems and slow development. Slow development may be very taxing for parents. For instance, babies born prematurely often are late to smile, to hold a bottle, and to communicate. And as time goes on, cognitive difficulties—either short- or long-term—may become evident.

Many children are born premature or weigh less than five pounds at birth. Some even have birth complications resulting in a diminished supply of oxygen for a period of time during delivery. Although prematurity, prolonged labor, and difficult deliveries are normal processes in human development, in the majority of instances they have no lasting adverse effect on an infant or a child. In fact, these days, most babies do not suffer any serious impairment during labor or at birth. Research shows that fewer than 10 percent of infants have any type of abnormality.

But two of the most common and important factors related to abnormalities are represented by prematurity and complications during delivery. That is, the most frequently seen birth complications are associated with anoxia (the lack of oxygen in the brain) and prematurity.

Premature infants are those born before they have completed the full term of pregnancy. Typically, full-term babies are born around the thirty-eighth week. A premature baby is almost always of low birth weight, although a baby can be born close to its due date but be of low birth weight.

Cerebral palsy becomes apparent weeks after birth. This is a disorder that results from damage to the brain's motor centers and which, later on, causes difficulties for the child in the areas of muscle control, and sometimes, speech. Cerebral palsy affects 20 percent of those babies who weighed less than thirty-five ounces (1,000 grams) at birth, 15 percent of those who weighed between two and three-and-a-half pounds, and 7 percent of those who weighed between three-and-a-half and five-and-a-half-pounds.

Babies who are born prematurely, or have a birth weight of less than five-and-a-half pounds, often have to stay in the hospital until they have gained weight while their vital functions are monitored to make sure there are no physical complications. Children can experience anoxia for various reasons during labor or during the birth process. However, one reason for anoxia is that the umbilical cord gets wrapped around the baby's neck, cutting off the oxygen supply to the infant's tissues. If a baby is deprived of oxygen for short periods of time, there may be only minor and temporary consequences, but if cut off from oxygen for long periods the baby will likely suffer serious complications.

Support for Parents Is Key

Many babies born in the United States are labeled as very low birth weight or extremely low birth weight; at the same time the median birth weight has been increasing. Also, simultaneously, the deaths of newborns have decreased sharply. This indicates, as research confirms, that the focus has been on saving the lives of the tiniest infants. Unfortunately, this intensive effort to save very tiny babies may be at the expense of providing greater resources toward prevention and failing to provide at-home care during early infancy.

Without such help in the early years, parents of children who are born prematurely or with low birth weight may feel overwhelmed by the special needs of a very tiny baby. Such babies are usually more demanding and less responsive than is a full-term baby who is full size. Research indicates that elevated rates of child abuse and neglect accompany the advances in saving premature and low birth weight babies. If those children are disabled as well, that can mean even greater susceptibility to abuse or neglect.

FACT

The best way to prevent vulnerable babies from abuse and to ease the burden of overwhelmed parents may be preventive medicine. That means ongoing education to prospective parents and the parents of newborn infants. Education encompasses nutrition for both mother and baby and help in gaining family and social support.

Factors That Aid Resilience

Which of the babies who suffer birth complications will have adverse effects lasting well beyond the infant years? That question was asked by researchers on the Hawaiian island of Kauai in the 1950s. So, a group of scientists led by Emmy Werner studied the effects of birth complications from an entire population of 698 children born on the island in 1955. Werner and her colleagues followed all of the people born that year, including the 10 percent who were born with some kind of handicap or anomaly.

What the researchers found was important and provided a great deal of hope for parents of children with birth complications. By following their subjects—these almost 700 children—for more than forty years, they discovered what kind of adults the at-risk youngsters would become. What they found had a lot to say about the environment in which children are raised.

For example, the study found that infants who had experienced severe birth complications but were living in stable families with high socioeconomic status and with mothers who had high intelligence, turned out to have IQs that did not essentially differ from children who had experienced no birth complications.

Furthermore, the most resilient children were those who had a resourceful approach to solving life's problems, who tended to view even their worst experiences in a positive light, who had the ability to gain positive attention from others, and who displayed a strong ability to use faith to maintain a positive vision of a meaningful life.

In effect, then, early complications tended to lessen in intensity or disappear altogether as some children grew up. If a child with early adversity was raised in a positive and nurturing environment with bright and loving parents, he was likely to make a successful adjustment.

As has been shown in many other studies since then, children who grow up in a family highlighted by a close and emotionally supportive relationship with caring adults become resilient. That means that children develop the capacity to achieve competence and satisfaction in life despite initially challenging or threatening circumstances.

Parents can't always protect their child from harm or complications—certainly not at birth. But they can do a lot to make sure that their children grow up knowing how to deal with even serious adversities.

CHAPTER 4

How the Brain Develops

This chapter will give you a more complete understanding of what the brain is at birth and how it develops into the more mature adolescent brain. Early brain growth is rapid and widespread. Children's brains need stimulation and a responsive environment to develop at an optimal rate. While various parts of the brain develop at differing rates, each stage of childhood and adolescence features different types of brain growth enabling children to acquire new skills as they grow. A focus for all adults should be on preventing unnecessary brain injuries. Making sure that children wear helmets when riding a bicycle is a minor example of the precautions parents and caregivers can take. But no matter what the activity, it is essential that kids be protected from the risk of injury to their most important asset.

How Does the Brain Develop?

The brain is an absolutely astounding organ in the human being. In fact, it is hard to imagine how the brain developed from the one-celled organism that was the embryo to become a functioning brain controlling the tiny body at birth. And even more miraculous is how many millions of connections there are in the brain of the newborn.

The brain and the nervous system of the child develop more rapidly than any other system in the body. By age seven, the brain is about the same weight and size as it will be when the person is an adult. But in order for the brain to attain that size, it must develop and grow. And grow it does.

The brain develops by the addition of neural pathways and connections among nerve cells. It used to be thought that when a child was born with a certain brain, that was it. The child was stuck with that particular brain. But, not so. The brain actually has considerable plasticity. And the development of the infant's brain depends on the environment and the experiences the child has. What children do and what they experience can change their brains.

The Brain at Birth

It is thanks to the brain and the parts of the brain that control basic processes—such as circulation, respiration, and consciousness—that the child is able to function outside of the womb, no longer connected to the mother, and able to live on his own.

FACT

When a child is born, the brain weighs about 350 grams, perhaps the size of a large baking potato. By the time a child reaches the age of one year, the brain has increased in size to about 1,400 grams.

While brain development occurs extensively during the prenatal period, it is much more substantial during infancy. But learning more about the brains of infants poses some problems. The latest brain-mapping technology cannot be used on babies. For example, positron-emission tomography

(PET) scans pose a radiation risk to babies. Also, infants are not very good at being still, so an MRI (magnetic resonance imaging) will not be much use. However, an EEG (electroencephalogram) can be used with infants to learn more about brain development during the first year. For instance, using EEGs, Charles Nelson and his colleagues have found that babies produce distinctive brain waves that reveal they can distinguish their mother's voice from another woman's voice.

The key developments during infancy and the first two years of life involve the myelin sheath. The myelin sheath is the layer of fat cells that speed up the electrical impulses along the axon and connections between dendrites. Dendrites receive information from the nerves, muscles, and glands. The cerebral cortex surrounds the rest of the brain and contains the greatest number of neurons and synapses. The development of cortical regions of the brain basically corresponds to the order in which various capacities emerge in the infant and growing child. For example, during the first year, auditory and visual cortexes develop. During the second and third year, there is rapid development in the language areas of the cerebral cortex. And throughout childhood and adolescence, the frontal lobes—which are responsible for many aspects of thinking, planning, and inhibiting impulses—are developing.

How Experiences Shape the Brain

Many parts of the brain depend on use in order to develop successfully. For instance, the cerebral cortex is greatly influenced by the experiences of the young child. The role of experiences in the development of neural pathways is demonstrated clearly by experiments with animals. When animals, particularly young animals, are stopped or prevented from using one sensory system or another in infancy, they can be permanently handicapped in that system. The sensory system, it has been found, is one system that is especially influenced by experiences. When an animal is denied sensory experiences, say, by being blindfolded in early life, it is never able to acquire normal vision. The implication of these animal experiments is that when infants are deprived cognitively and socially, there can be far-reaching implications. Severe deprivation of a child in the early years of life may well prevent future normal brain development.

Brain Development in Early Childhood

Throughout childhood the brain continues to develop by adding connections between neurons and by the process of **myelination**. Myelination is a process in which neural fibers are coated with an insulating fatty sheath called myelin, which improves the efficiency of message transfer. With the continuing changes in the brain, children become able to plan their actions, attend to stimuli more effectively, and make considerable strides in language development.

Both the brain and the head surrounding the brain grow more rapidly than any other part of the body. Some of the brain's increase in size is due to myelination, but growth of the brain is also associated with the number and size of dendrites.

Some child development specialists contend that myelination is important in the maturation of a number of abilities in children, for instance, eye-hand coordination. Myelination in the areas of the brain related to eye-hand coordination may not be complete until the child is about four years of age. Some research, using MRIs with children around four years of age, found that those children who were described as being delayed in their motor and cognitive milestones had significantly reduced levels of myelination. Furthermore, looking at another ability—that of focusing attention—studies show that myelination of those areas of the brain related to being able to focus attention is not complete until middle or late childhood.

FACT

There is proportionally more growth that takes place in the head and the brain than in any other part of the body. Anatomical changes in the child's brain between the ages of three and fifteen may be dramatic, but it is in the local patterns that change occurs. For instance, there is rapid growth at different times in the frontal lobe areas and somewhat later in the temporal and parietal lobes. All of these periods of growth lead to the development of different skills and abilities.

Overall, the brain grows in fits and starts. That is, using brain scans of young children over several years, researchers have found that the brains of children experience rapid and distinct periods of growth. During the years from three to six, the most rapid growth occurs in the frontal lobe areas. The frontal lobe is involved in planning and organizing new actions and in maintaining attention to tasks. Then, from age six to puberty, the most dramatic growth occurs in the temporal and parietal lobes. These parts of the brain are involved in language and spatial relations.

Recent research by Diamond, Casey, and Munakata found that children after about age seven show increased efficiency in cognitive control. This would involve flexible and effective control in a number of skills or abilities—controlling attention, reducing interfering thoughts, inhibiting motor activities, and switching between competing choices with flexibility.

Brain Development in Adolescence

Everything is in a state of motion with teenagers. Their bodies are rapidly changing, their voices are changing, their emotions are in a state of flux. And their brains are changing, too. But how much is the adolescent brain changing? And in what ways is it changing? Some psychologists would contend that knowledge of the teenage brain is in its infancy. Simply put, psychologists don't know that much about how the adolescent brain is developing. But what do they know?

Psychologists certainly know that pruning takes place. Throughout childhood and adolescence, a process called pruning is constantly happening. And what this means is that early in life there are dramatic increases in the dendrites and synapses of the brain. But nearly twice as many of these connections in the brain are made than will ever be used. When connections are used, they are strengthened and survive; when they are not used, they are replaced by other pathways and the original connects disappear. That is, connections that go unused are lost in a process called pruning.

What results from this pruning is that by the end of adolescence, the individual has fewer, more selective, and more effective neuronal connections than he had as a child. However, those neural connections that remain suggest what the adolescent has chosen to engage in or not to engage in.

Along with pruning, there is, scientists have recently discovered, significant structural change in the brain that occurs during the teen years. For instance, the **corpus callosum**, the part of the brain where fibers connect the brain's right and left hemispheres, thickens during the teen years. That improves the teen's ability to process information.

Throughout childhood and adolescence, there is development of the **prefrontal cortex**. As indicated earlier, the prefrontal cortex is the highest level of the frontal lobes, which are involved in decision making, reasoning, and self-control. While there is constant development in this area of the brain, the prefrontal cortex doesn't finish maturing for several years.

On the other hand, there is a part of the brain called the **amygdala**, the seat of the emotions, which matures earlier than the prefrontal cortex. This is why the emotions of teens may overwhelm their common sense, their reasoning, or their judgment.

Teenagers differ from adults in the way they behave, the way they solve problems, and the way they make decisions. It is known that even in late adolescence the brain is still continuing to grow and develop. The amygdala, which is responsible for instinctual reactions including fear and aggressive behavior, develops early. But the frontal cortex—the area of the brain that controls reasoning and helps people think before they act—develops much later.

Teenagers and the Amygdala

Teenagers' actions are guided more by the amygdala and less by the frontal cortex. This means that adolescents are more likely to act on impulse, misread or misinterpret social cues and emotions, get into accidents of all kinds, and engage in dangerous or risky behavior. They may even be more likely to react with **aggression** or anger.

On the other hand, given the uneven development of the amygdala and the frontal cortex, they are less likely to think before they act, consider all the consequences of their actions, or modify dangerous or inappropriate behavior.

In a study published by Sarah Whittle and her associates in a report of the *National Academy of Sciences* in 2008, the research team measured the volume of the amygdala and the frontal cortex in adolescents and compared the size of those parts of the brain to reports of teens' interactions with their parents. What these researchers found was that adolescents who maintained their aggressive emotions longest during a conflict with their parents were consistently found to have larger amygdala volume.

What this finding by Whittle and her colleagues suggests is that when the development of the prefrontal cortex in teens is delayed—or has not caught up with amygdala development—adolescents will be more unreasonable and even aggressive in trying to resolve conflicts with their parents. Wait a few years for the frontal cortex to catch up and the same teens may be much more adult-like in their ability to solve problems with their parents.

When Does the Brain Become Mature?

Brain maturation does not stop at age seven or ten or even fifteen. It continues into the late teens and even into the twenties. Research over the last decade or more at the National Institute of Mental Health, often through the use of MRIs, has determined that the adolescent brain is a work in progress.

Up until recently, psychologists and scientists thought the major wiring of the brain was completed by as early as age three and that the brain was fully mature by the start of adolescence. But the more recent findings suggest otherwise. The greatest changes to the prefrontal cortex do not occur prior to adolescence. In fact, the frontal cortex is continuing to grow and change into early adulthood. That means that the functions associated with the prefrontal cortex—self-control, judgment, and organization—develop most between puberty and adulthood.

ESSENTIAL

People are more likely to have a mature brain in their mid-twenties. That's when their thinking will be more purposeful and when their brains are more likely to put the brakes on their emotions.

If parents, educators, and even policy makers assume that teenagers are mature in mind as well as in body, then they may completely misunderstand how adolescents function. Everyone who deals with teens should understand there is a reason why teens often fail to listen to adults or heed warnings about their choices and risky behaviors. The reason is that the immature brains of adolescents often are just not capable of understanding adults and of thinking in rational, logical ways while taking into consideration all of the potential negative consequences of their actions.

Risk Factors in Brain Development

What gets in the way of and interferes with normal brain development? The answer is that there are various kinds of abnormalities that can occur in infancy, childhood, and even in adolescence. Perhaps the abnormality that has been studied the most is retardation.

Mental retardation in the United States occurs in between 1 and 2 percent of the population. Mental retardation, or developmental disability, is defined as "significantly sub-average intellectual functioning" by the American Association of Intellectual and Developmental Disabilities. About 25 percent of individuals designated as mentally retarded or developmentally disabled have an identifiable physical origin to their disability. These physical origins can include several kinds of inherited disorders and brain damage.

Many of the chromosomal anomalies, such as Down syndrome, are typically accompanied by mild or moderate retardation. A child may also inherit a specific disease or inborn error of metabolism, which can cause retardation if not treated. The best known such inherited metabolism error is PKU.

FACT

Children with PKU lack the liver enzymes needed to digest the amino acid phenylalanine. A metabolic chain reaction is set in motion that results in brain damage, hyperactivity, and mental retardation. About 1 in every 15,000 births results in a child with PKU.

Another physical cause of retardation is brain damage. Brain damage, in general, can result from a large number of causes. These causes include diseases in the mother during pregnancy, such as rubella or syphilis, both of which can produce damage to the brain of the fetus. Also, severe malnutrition during pregnancy can injure a fetus' brain. Furthermore, maternal alcoholism has the potential for causing damage to the developing brain of a fetus. In addition, an infant's brain can be damaged during delivery or by some accident after birth. A fall from a bed, a high chair, or a car accident can all result in significant damage to the young brain.

The other 75 percent of individuals with developmental disability show no signs of any brain damage or physical causes. The brain damage in this group of children and teens may have come from families in which parents have low IQs themselves, where there is serious family dysfunction, where there is mental illness, or where there is extreme emotional or cognitive deprivation in the home.

Building Better Brains: What Parents Can Do

Building a better brain doesn't involve buying DVDs to make a child's brain like Einstein's. Nor does it require parents to play Mozart while the fetus is developing in the womb. In fact, there is no research that these approaches will result in the super genius many parents might like their child to become.

But research does show that children who grow up in deprived environments may also suffer from deprived brain growth. Rene Spitz, an American psychiatrist, studied children raised in orphanages during the 1940s. What he observed and documented was that children who were raised in unresponsive and nonstimulating orphanages became depressed.

However, children who are in nonstimulating and nonresponsive environments also have depressed *brain* activity. In fact, child development researchers are questioning whether there is any recoverability or reversibility of the damage done to a young brain from such deprivation.

In effect, a young child's brain is just waiting for experiences in order that new connections in the brain can take place. But after birth, if there is not a steady stream of sights, sounds, smells, touch, language, and eye contact, then the brain is not able to form new connections. Without new connections and without the wiring that new stimulations and experiences bring about, the brain suffers.

Parents and caregivers have to make sure that the environment of children, starting at the moment of birth, is stimulating and constantly interesting.

Providing a rich environment creates neural connections and helps to generate brain activity.

Children and Accidents

In the United States, accidents are by far the major cause of childhood deaths. In the United States, a child has about a 1 in 600 chance of dying due to an accident before age fifteen. This is about four times the risk of dying from cancer.

About two-thirds of accidental deaths among preschool children are related to such accidents as falling, drowning, choking, and poisoning. This means that parents ought to be concerned about injury control. Injury control, according to Kathleen Berger, author of the book *The Developing Person Through the Life Span*, means to take precautions to prevent as many injuries as possible and to reduce the harm done by those accidents that do occur.

While children, especially preschool children, do not always have the brain development to take preventive actions to forestall injuries to themselves, parents and adults can use forethought in order to safeguard children. That safeguarding often requires adult supervision of young children—and even adolescents. For example, children under two years of age, especially those that are just beginning to crawl and move around their environment, need to be watched constantly. Young children should not be left alone for even a moment as they do not have sufficient brain development to understand the risks and the dangers.

ESSENTIAL

Other safety precautions parents and caregivers can take include making sure all medicine containers have childproof-safety caps, making sure clothing—particularly sleepwear—is flame-retardant, making sure there are fences around pools and lakes, fencing in dogs that might bite a child, and making sure all firearms are locked up.

To prevent accidents, parents and caregivers should take safety measures to help protect children. Such measures could involve locking windows that can be reached by children, removing cleaning products to a spot that children cannot access, or making sure that a medicine cabinet is locked or inaccessible to young children.

Protecting the Brain of a Child

Beyond protecting children from the potentially devastating effects of injury, there are safety measures and precautions that parents and caregivers can take to safeguard children from accidents. Although children can't be protected from all accidents, there are things parents can do specifically to protect the heads and brains of children and teens.

For example, the most obvious thing parents can do is to insist that children wear helmets and headgear when bicycling. The greater use of helmets has resulted in 88 percent fewer head and brain injuries in recent years. Children's heads should be protected in almost every sport or athletic event. For instance, children should not be encouraged to use their head to hit the ball in soccer because those headbutts may result in damage—however minimal one or two headers might be thought to be—to young brains. Other sports, such as baseball, football, motorcross, skateboarding, snowboarding, and several other sports should use the best available headgear to protect children from concussions.

In general, though, parents and caregivers can help make sure the precious brains of children are protected by being aware of the multitude of situations that could result in a head injury. Whether it is riding in a car (and making sure the child safety seat or booster seat is properly manufactured and installed correctly) or engaging in various other day-to-day activities, supervision by adults is the first, most important thing to be done to protect children's brains.

CHAPTER 5

The Growing and Developing Infant

Infancy is the period from the moment of birth until around one year of age or slightly later. Babies, it has been discovered, have many physical and cognitive capabilities immediately. Among the skills that are apparent at birth or soon thereafter are memory, all of the sensory experiences, and cognitive skills. In other words, a baby is not a blank slate. Instead, infants come into the world with some very basic skills and by the time they are one year of age they have gained remarkable skills and their cognitive development is amazing.

How Do Infants Perceive the World?

Do newborns even have the ability to see you and their environments? While some baby animals cannot see at all for several days after birth, newborn humans are born with the physiological readiness to see what's going on around them and to respond to what they see. However, in the first month of life, babies do not have visual acuity. That is, they do not have sharp, clear vision. They can detect changes in brightness, they can distinguish movement, and they can track a moving object with their eyes. But unless an object is held up to them or unless a parent is within a few inches of their eyes, most things are going to appear blurry and indistinct. Visual acuity, though, improves markedly over the first few weeks and months after birth. And between six months and twelve months, babies' visual acuity improves so much that their ability to see is almost like the visual acuity of an adult.

Do babies see in color? The answer to this is that they probably don't see much in color during the first month, but certainly by two months infants are beginning to respond to color. By three months, researchers have determined that their color vision is working just fine, but their depth perception is not so great. However, give them another two or three months and their overall vision is functioning quite remarkably well.

Do Babies Recognize Their Parents?

During those first few weeks and months are babies able to see and recognize their parents? At first, since their vision is blurry, they won't actually see their parents that clearly. But give them a few weeks and they will be looking their mothers and fathers in the eyes and they will be fascinated by how their parents look.

But there's more to seeing their world than what babies visualize with their eyes. Actually, normal, full-term babies enter the world with all the sensory systems functioning. But, as with their vision, not all sensory capacities are at the same level of maturity at birth.

The Hearing of Infants

Aside from having fluid in their ears at first, newborns have hearing that is fairly mature. Make a loud noise and an infant—even one that is only a few minutes old—will startle and may even cry. If the noise isn't too loud or scary, infants will turn their heads toward the source of the noise.

Babies appear able to distinguish the sound of the human voice from other kinds of sound. Studies strongly suggest that infants prefer the sound of the human voice over most other sounds. There is also evidence that some babies as young as four days show they have a preference for the language spoken around them over a foreign language.

In general, while their hearing is fairly acute, it will continue to mature over a few weeks to be just as acute as the hearing of an older child or an adult.

When it comes to taste and smell, newborns have well-developed senses. Not only are newborns sensitive to odors, but they can tell one odor from another. Their sense of taste is also acute, and it is clear that most babies prefer sweet to sour tastes.

Babies and Their Tactile Senses

Babies react to touch. Touch a baby on his foot and he will reflexively jerk his foot. And infants also respond to temperature changes. For example, they can sense and they will react to a sudden drop in the temperature. Infants also respond to abrupt changes in their physical position. For instance, if they are suddenly tipped up or dropped, they will respond with distinctive, reflex-like movements.

Infant Cognitive Development

There is remarkable physical development taking place throughout infancy. But just as remarkably, there are changes in the baby's capacity to understand and relate to the world. Although it may not be apparent, newborns already have some cognitive skills. But by the time a child is two years of age, consider what they can do:

- They can use language to express feelings, needs, and perceptions.
- They can solve problems by applying several solutions.

- They can remember what has happened in the past.
- They can anticipate the future.
- They can think about what happened in the past.

The growth and change in a baby's mental capacity that began at birth and continues through adolescence is called cognitive development. Cognitive abilities are those that require thinking and learning and involve memory, problem solving, concept formation, and language acquisition. Put all these cognitive functions together into an integrated system and you have the concept of intelligence.

There is much that babies can do besides eat, sleep, and eliminate waste products. In fact, a baby can: blink at bright lights, focus on people or objects between 8 and 12 inches away, turn toward the direction of sound, distinguish volume and pitch of sounds, prefer high-toned voices, distinguish tastes, prefer sweet-tasting beverages, and grasp and grip a finger or an object if her hand accidently touches it.

Learning and Memory

It is difficult to talk about the acquisition of knowledge or behavior change through learning without discussing memory. It may well be said that learning and memory very much depend on each other.

First, an infant must learn information in order to remember that information or those facts. But it is memory that provides evidence that learning has occurred. During infancy, two things happen in terms of memory:

1. The baby remembers things for a longer period of time.
2. As the baby acquires more experience, he accumulates more memories.

One of the milestone accomplishments in cognitive development during the first year of life is an infant's ability to think using representations of language and other symbols. But, in general, basic learning processes appear to be present very early in life. What changes over the course of development seems to be the nature of the information that babies are capable of learning and, perhaps, the speed and efficiency with which they learn.

Psychologists say there are three kinds of learning behaviors in infants:

- Classical conditioning
- Operant conditioning
- Imitative learning

Classical conditioning refers to a type of learning in which individuals learn to respond to unfamiliar stimuli in the same way they respond to familiar stimuli. For example, babies as young as two hours old can learn to associate a stroke on the head with being able to suck on a sugary beverage. Eventually, the stroke on the head elicits the same kind of puckering and sucking response that initially came about only when sucking on the sugary substance.

Operant conditioning means learning to emit or inhibit some behavior because of the rewarding (or punishing) consequences it will bring. A newborn's smile can be brought about simply by hearing the sound of the mother's voice.

Imitative learning means that babies can also learn by observing the behaviors of parents, siblings, or other people and then doing the same thing. This is imitation and it begins early in life—maybe even in the first few days after birth.

ESSENTIAL

Andrew Meltzoff and M. Keith Moore reported in the journal *Child Development* in 1983 that they conducted studies in which they found that babies between the ages of seven and seventy-two hours following birth were able to imitate adults who opened their mouths very wide or stuck out their tongues.

By eight or nine months babies can engage in true imitation. For example, researchers have noted that nine-month-olds can push a set of buttons or shake objects that make a noise after watching someone else do these things first. What's more, not only can they carry out these imitations immediately after seeing them, but also the imitation can occur twenty-four hours later with no opportunity to practice the behaviors in between. At fourteen months, children can delay their imitation for one week. And between fourteen and eighteen months old, they can not only delay their imitation but they can repeat an action in a completely different situation.

Babies and Memory

Even very young infants can remember what they see and hear after various time spans. Researchers have found that newborns can remember a previously seen event over a twenty-four-hour time period. Other studies show that newborns can remember speech sounds for as much as one day. Three-month-olds have been taught to make a mobile move by kicking it. Four weeks later, placed in a similar situation, they can remember to kick the mobile to see it move.

The result of many studies by many scientists leads to the conclusion that between birth and three months babies can remember a great deal of what goes on in their lives or what they have been taught.

Crying and Distress

How much do babies cry? In a study done by well-known pediatrician T. Berry Brazelton, mothers were asked to keep daily records of their infants' crying for the first twelve weeks of life. The study showed that crying increased from an hour and forty-five minutes per day at two weeks of age to a peak of two hours and forty-five minutes per day at six weeks of age. Then, the crying diminished gradually to less than an hour a day by twelve weeks of age.

Researchers have also found that young infants cried at various times throughout the day and night, but there is a strong tendency for infants to cry between 6 P.M. and 11 P.M.

Crying is one of the earliest means of communicating for babies. In the early weeks and months, the crying of infants is related to physical needs: hunger, hiccups, or digestive problems. By three to four months, crying is less associated with physical distress and increasingly related to the baby's psychological needs. Also, by three to four months most infants spend less of their day crying, and are easier to soothe.

When babies cry because they are hungry or wet, they can generally be soothed by solving the problem with a feeding or a dry diaper. When crying continues for no apparent reason, the term "fussing" is generally used to describe the ongoing crying. When parents can't readily relieve the crying of the fussy baby the parents become frustrated.

ALERT

In cases of extreme fussiness, the baby is often said to have "colic." Colic consists of bursts of irritability, fussing, or crying that lasts for more than three hours a day. Fussy and extremely fussy babies also tend to be more sensitive, more irritable, and less easily soothed than average, and they are more than usually active. While many factors have been suggested as reasons for colic, there's no scientific evidence that points to one cause.

What Are Babies Thinking?

Do babies think? The simple answer is yes. But to make things more complex, it depends on how you define *thinking*.

One definition of thinking, according to John Santrock in his book *Child Development*, is that thinking is manipulating and transforming information in memory, usually to form concepts, reason critically, and solve problems. Given this definition, it is clear that infants do form concepts. The problem is that child development specialists and child psychologists just don't know how early concept formation begins.

Some researchers have found that babies as young as three months of age can group together objects with similar appearances. Some very young children develop an intense, passionate interest in a particular category of objects or activities. In a 2007 study published in *Developmental Psychology* researchers discovered a large **gender** difference in categories, with an intense interest in particular categories stronger for boys than girls. Boys focused on vehicles, trains, machines, dinosaurs, and balls. Girls' intense interests were more focused on dress-up, books, and reading.

Because infants don't have language, no one really knows what a baby is thinking throughout the day. They are thinking something; it's just not known exactly what.

The Emotional Development of Infants

Emotions are the feeling tone with which individuals respond to their surroundings and their circumstances. Emotions are not simply feelings, but rather processes by which individuals establish, maintain, and terminate relations between themselves and others.

No matter how emotions are defined, they are an important aspect of human psychological functioning. In interviews with mothers of very young children—some as young as four weeks of age—the mothers reported a high incidence of distinct emotional expression. The mothers reported that they interpreted what their infants needed based on the emotions they expressed. Among the emotions the mothers claimed their babies expressed were interest, joy, surprise, fear, and sadness.

ESSENTIAL

The evidence that newborns express emotions is indirect. Psychologists depend on the assumption that infants will reveal their emotions through facial expressions, noises, and movements.

What do emotions do for children?

- They help children survive and adapt to their environment.
- They help to guide and motivate children's behavior.
- They support communication with others.

A majority of psychologists contend that one thing is clear: infants have emotions. Carroll E. Izard, a professor of psychology in the Human Emotions Laboratory at the University of Delaware, has been a central figure in the study of children's emotional development. Like other developmental specialists, Izard contends that each emotion has its own distinctive facial pattern. Over decades of research, Izard has found that babies have intense feelings from the moment of birth. In fact, Izard has written, babies' inner feelings are limited to distress, disgust, and interest at first. But as they mature, new emotions, often one or two at a time, develop in an orderly fashion.

For example, infants gain the social smile (suggesting the emotion of joy) at around four to six weeks; begin to express anger, surprise, and sadness at around three to four months; show fear at five to seven months; display shame, shyness and self-awareness at about six to eight months; and express contempt and guilt during the second year of life.

Not all psychologists agree entirely with Izard, but few, if any, psychologists argue that infants have no emotions. It's simply a matter as to when emotions emerge. Do they develop in an orderly manner as Izard contends? Or are they present at birth?

Separation Anxiety and Object Permanence

Separation anxiety refers to the distress registered by infants when a key attachment figure leaves. And this usually happens between eight and twelve months of age. Then, attached children may become concerned when their chief caregiver departs for any length of time. They register their displeasure by crying, withdrawing, and rejecting alternative care. Separation anxiety seems to reach a peak at the age of about eighteen months.

ESSENTIAL

Infant separation anxiety is related to the mother's or the key caregiver's parenting style. In particular, separation anxiety is related to the parent's responsiveness to the baby's physical and emotional needs.

According to Jerome Kagan, a pioneering developmental psychologist and professor emeritus of psychology at Harvard University, children react to separation with anxiety because they are faced with discrepant or unfamiliar events that they cannot understand or correct. In effect, what happens is that mother (or another essential caregiver) leaves and with the disappearance the infant's feelings of comfort and pleasure disappear as well.

If a child is eight or nine months of age, the infant is not capable of taking any comfort in the fact that the parent will return. That's because **object permanence** (the concept that an object exists even if out of the child's presence or out of her sight) does not develop in children until about the tenth month. By age two, separation anxiety subsides since the child is better able to recognize the permanence of parental figures and is much better able to tolerate frustration.

Parents often assume that prompt responsiveness to the baby's cries will produce a whiney, overly demanding infant who will not be able to tolerate separation. But just the opposite is true. Prompt, appropriate response to the baby's signals will increase the child's confidence in the parent's accessibility and responsiveness. The more confidence and trust the child has in the parent, the more easily the child can accept brief separation. Instead of crying when the mother leaves, the confident child will greet Mom or Dad happily when they return.

Stranger Fears and Inhibitions

In new and novel situations, many children between one and three years show by their facial expression how they feel. They look sober or worried, may drop their eyes, or they may grab on to their parents or even hide behind either Mom or Dad. At times, if the situation is unlike anything they've encountered before, they may even whimper or cry.

QUESTION

Should I be concerned because my twenty-one-month-old daughter seems fearful of strangers?
Toddlers between ages one and three years typically develop into buoyant and exuberant little people, full of life and energy. But toddlers are also capable of quiet reserve. This is most likely to happen when they encounter the unfamiliar. At home they feel confident as they are irrepressible and quick to let their parents know what they like—and what they don't like. But outside of home or in the presence of a stranger, they can be reserved, quiet, even fearful.

All toddlers react like this at one time or another. For some, though, it may be an attempt to process what is going on that may last for twenty or thirty minutes before they start to feel more relaxed and begin to act like the exuberant tyke they normally are. Jerome Kagan, the Harvard developmental psychologist and author, has been researching the social life of young children for decades. Kagan believes that about 20 percent of American children exhibit an extreme form of timidity and shyness.

For Kagan, these are children who show more of an "inhibition to the unfamiliar." Other psychologists have referred to these children as having a set of temperamental traits that make them slow to warm up to new situations or people. Such slow-to-warm-up little kids are shy with strangers, cautious when exposed to new objects, and timid in new situations.

Kagan has studied whether children who have this reserve, timidity, and inhibition continue to be like this in later years of childhood or if they carry these characteristics even into adulthood. He's found that only about half of the extremely reserved and inhibited toddlers go on to be shy and timid older children or adults who are not very outgoing.

CHAPTER 6

The Toddler Years

Mention the word *toddler* and many people will instantly think "the terrible twos." But toddlers, those children between the ages of about one and four years, are about so much more than temper tantrums. The toddler years are about rapid development, the transition from babyhood to childhood, about excitement, enthusiasm, energy, and, yes, about opposition and temper tantrums. But this is not a terrible stage of development at all, particularly if parents and caregivers know what to expect.

What Is a Toddler?

A toddler is a young child who has just graduated from being an infant and has gone into the next stage of development. Toddlers look and act very different from the baby who was so dependent on her parents. It was only at the end of the infancy stage that babies began to get around by crawling. Now that they are toddlers they are completely mobile. They can walk—tentatively at first—and then before long, they are running. With mobility comes freedom.

And if the child did not seem to be curious before, she likely is now. Toddlers typically want to examine everything and they want to know as much as possible about their environment. That means they will get into cupboards, cabinets, drawers, and whatever they can reach. They want to check out everything they see—including the family pet and the electric outlets.

They definitely have a personality at this point and they will express how they feel. Since they are now in the flush of who they are, they don't want to be controlled by anyone. Toddlers want independence and freedom. Now, they are likely to say "No!" if you ask them a question. They want to be their own persons and that means resisting doing what their parents want them to do. Ask them to come to you and they're likely to run in the other direction. Give them two choices and they're likely to pick one, then change to the second, and then cry if they don't get both.

The toddler has made tremendous strides from being a dependent baby to an energetic and active toddler. Because of both mobility and language, the toddler exerts a strong presence in her environment. But this presence is made even stronger by her insistence that she be independent and autonomous. The toddler wants to do things on her own—even when she is not quite capable of acting like her own person.

This desire for independence leads to clashes with parents who want to protect her from her own curiosity and impulsive behavior. These clashes can become drawn-out temper tantrums or stubborn power struggles. The wise parent learns to sidestep power struggles, to use positive discipline techniques to avoid being repressive, and to provide toddlers with responsive and sensitive care, which allows for a secure attachment relationship between parent and child. In the long run, a secure attachment will help the toddler learn to better regulate her emotions.

The Physical Development of a Toddler

Toddlers between the ages of one year and two years are usually delightful because of their general zest, friendliness, and agreeableness. At this stage of development, young children are able to exert greater control over their environment through the acquisition of language and especially with the addition of the word "no." But they also have much better control of their motor skills and are often surprisingly quick in their ability to get around. As a result, they are usually in need of almost constant supervision.

From twenty-four to thirty-six months of age, toddlers are often friendly, curious, active, and what might be called "eager beavers." At times the toddler at this stage seems to be going in many different directions all at once; sometimes it seems as if her activities are out of control. Physically, she is often clumsy and inexpert at many things she tries.

Three-year-old toddlers are somewhat more compliant (often, but certainly not always!). They have a better ability to walk and run, and their balance is much improved. Some are riding bicycles, albeit sometimes with training wheels. And they often show they can use a remote control, play a DVD, or use the CD player—usually much to the chagrin of their parents. And they can use their greater physical mobility to cause concern. Not only can they open the refrigerator, but they may think they can handle a quart of milk to fix their own bowl of cereal, at times with disastrous or comic results. They can climb up into cupboards and they can get into things that they couldn't reach in past months. Again, this means that with their greater mobility they have to be supervised very closely.

Cognitive Development During the Toddler Years

A truly extraordinary amount of language development occurs between the end of infancy—when many children will be speaking either no words or just a limited few—and the end of the toddler years, when it is not unusual for three- or four-year-olds to have a vocabulary of a thousand words. So a toddler of three or four is vastly superior to the one-year-old in terms of his communication skills. In other words, the older child is increasingly able to receive, transmit, and otherwise manipulate information about the world around him.

With an ability to learn by absorbing information conveyed to him in various ways, with his ability to transmit information to others, and with his ability to communicate with himself, the toddler experiences profound changes in his cognitive life.

With infants, they understand the world and their environment basically by perceiving it and acting on it. But toddlers can do so much more. They can select information, store it in their memory, and retrieve it when they want to use it. They can classify and order objects. And they can imagine the consequences of an action without actually carrying out the contemplated action.

Toddlers are really thinking during these years. Every parent of a two- or three-year-old has seen this. When a parent instructs a two- or three-year-old not to do something, the adult is likely to get a stare and the parent has a good idea about what's going on in the toddler's mind. It is probably a variation on this thought: "If I do it anyway, what is he going to do about it?" And the toddler does it anyway, daring his parent to do something about it.

At other times their thinking is related to their ability to consider the rules. For instance, some three-year-olds are fully aware of the rules and when they approach a situation where a rule applies, they may speak aloud to themselves: "Brittany, be nice to the baby."

Learning to Talk

Between three and seven months after birth most babies begin to babble. Babbling is the repetition of consonant and vowel combinations, such as "gagaga" or "bababa." Infants all over the world use the same sounds when they begin to babble. Those sounds later become very specific words, such as *mama* for mother or *baba* for bottle or drink.

As sounds acquire meaning, infants begin to practice speech sounds common to their culture, with other sounds less common in their culture falling from use.

The Toddler's First Words

During the first year of life, youngsters go from no words to a vocabulary. Usually in the second half of the first year they start babbling and playing with sounds. By age twelve months or so, some words are almost there as they imitate what their parents are communicating to them. Then, from twelve to twenty-four months, they often say their first word. It may be "dada" or "mama," but the word is there and once said, it gets repeated often.

FACT

Of all children, 7 percent talk before they are eight months of age, while 2 percent do not attempt to use words until after age two. There seems to be no difference in later speech development between those who spoke their words early and those who spoke their first words later.

That first word leads to other words and between ages two and three, new words seem to come about weekly or even daily. With a vocabulary of about fifty words during the second year, the increase in words—even multisyllabic words—grows at an amazing rate. At around two to two-and-a-half, the words get combined together. First in two-word utterances such as "my baby" or "me go," and then three- and four-word sentences such as "Me not want to."

How Toddlers Play

In the second half of the first year of life truly social behavior begins to appear. Infants, for instance, begin to recognize a peer as a social partner. But during the second year, children make terrific strides in locomotion and language, and these strides make social exchange much more possible.

In the early toddler period (thirteen to twenty-four months), children develop the capacity to engage in social interaction that can be complementary. That is, young toddlers can exchange both turns and roles. They begin to be involved in one another's activities. And they are more likely to smile or laugh with each other or show other kinds of appropriate social affect.

In the late toddler period (twenty-five to thirty-six months), the main social achievement is the ability to share meaning within a social partnership. However, this does not mean that they are playing together in the sense that older children might play together. During the toddler years, they are more likely to be engaging in parallel play. Parallel play means that they are playing side by side, even at the same activity (such as playing in a sand box or drawing at the same table), but there is no interaction or turn-taking going on.

QUESTION

My thirty-month-old son gets into fights with other children during play dates. Should I be worried when he hits and bites other children?
As children develop during the toddler years, negative exchanges and conflict often increase. But at this stage of development, children don't know how to avoid conflict, they don't know how to control their impulsivity and their emotions, and they certainly don't know how to resolve a conflict. They become more civil as they improve in their social skills.

What Toddlers Need from Parents

One of the priorities of the parent-child relationship is the development of a secure attachment between child and parent. In order that a secure attachment takes place, the parent must provide certain things.

First, a young child needs affection and physical contact. Second, a child needs acceptance, not rejection. Third, a child requires that parents be available to meet their needs. That is, young children need parents who will be responsive to their signals and constantly and consistently meeting the needs expressed by those signals. In order to be responsive to the child's ongoing needs, parents must be both physically and emotionally available to their child. Fourth, and perhaps summarizing all of the various needs of toddlers, they need "sensitive care" from their parents. This means they need parenting and care that leads to a secure attachment relationship.

How the Quality of Attachment Affects Toddlers

Attachment is the relationship or bond between parent and child that develops out of the interaction between a parent and child. It is important that an early, secure attachment develops out of the interaction between them. Research shows that an early secure attachment is related to more complex exploratory behavior when a toddler is about two years old.

With security and a great curiosity comes an intense interest and enjoyment in solving problems. This positive approach to problem-solving is seldom seen in toddlers who were insecurely attached as infants. Some researchers have found that securely attached two-year-olds are more likely to be enthusiastic, persistent, cooperative, and effective in solving problems then are insecurely attached children.

Securely attached toddlers engage in more symbolic pretend play and more high-level symbolic play. In addition, securely attached toddlers generally show more positive emotions in their day-to-day life, and they seem to have greater empathy for others along with a more advanced ability to initiate interactions with other people. Securely attached children tend to whine less, are less apprehensive, and display fewer negative reactions than insecurely attached toddlers.

With secure attachment comes a better understanding of emotions in children. Attachment to the mother allows young children to process emotional information, understand emotions, and regulate their emotions. When children are better at regulating their emotions, they are in a much better position to form excellent social relationships.

Handling Temper Tantrums

The age of temper tantrums is between ages two and five, with the number of tantrums decreasing after age five. Toddlers get frustrated because they are not expert at self-regulation yet. They are in the process of learning to regulate their emotions, but they are not there yet. Therefore, when they are told "no," when limits are put on them, or they don't get immediately what they desire, they may have an emotional meltdown—the famed toddler temper tantrum.

Here are the steps to successfully handling a tantrum:

1. Don't try to stop the tantrum.
2. Don't give in to the tantrum by giving the child what she wants.
3. Protect the child and valuable property; one way to do this is to remove a child from the scene of the tantrum to a safe and, if possible, sparsely furnished place.
4. Ignore the tantrum until it runs its course.
5. When the tantrum is over, resume life as if nothing happened.

Although there is little preventive action that parents can take when a tantrum is in full anger mode, there are actions that can be taken at other times that will help reduce tantrums over time. For instance, parents can give verbal praise when a child accepts the word "no" or deals with frustration successfully. Parents can let her know, as part of the praise, what she did well to be successful. Furthermore, they can teach her skills to be calm when she is becoming frustrated or angry. And they can teach a young child problem-solving skills to replace the temper tantrums.

Dealing with the Emotions of a Toddler

Toddlers are learning to regulate their emotions. Therefore, they will show many emotions in addition to those associated with temper tantrums. Part of being a responsive parent is to help the toddler handle his emotions in appropriate ways.

The first thing that can be done is to help a child acknowledge his emotions; for example, when a child is frustrated because he is having trouble with a situation, a parent can say, "It is so frustrating when the puppy won't let you pet him, isn't it?"

The second thing that can be done is help him put his feelings into words: "When you are frustrated because Jason won't let you play with the toy, tell him how you feel. Say to Jason, 'I'm getting frustrated because you won't let me play with the fire truck.'"

The third aspect of learning to help a young child deal successfully with his emotions is to begin to teach elementary principles of conflict resolution or problem solving. A parent could say, "I know it is frustrating when you can't play with a toy when you want, but let's think of what else you could do instead. Could you play with another toy until Jason is done playing with the truck?"

By gradually increasing the instructions for solving problems, a young child learns there are alternative ways of solving problems, aside from having a meltdown or using anger or aggressive actions.

ALERT

The toddler is much more inclined than the infant to be independent and autonomous. Toddlers now have language on their side with which they can express themselves. The two-year-old often lets parents know what they want by boldly declaring "I do it!" or "I want to!" Often, parents see the once friendly and usually fairly tranquil child turn into a demon who becomes bossy, demanding, and temperamental.

Handing the Need for Independence and Autonomy

Because toddlers, especially around age two-and-a-half, will assert their independence—usually with the most-often used word in their limited vocabulary: "No!"—parents should be prepared. Parenting and caregiving works much more smoothly when adults expect this behavior and are prepared to deal with it comfortably. The best way to handle the independence and the oppositional behavior of the toddler is by not overreacting to their demands for independence or their need to go against what adults want. A toddler's "nos" should be ignored as much as possible.

Giving an order, trying to force a child to do or say what the adult wants, or making a threat, will set up a power struggle. It is better to try to lead or guide the toddler in the right direction rather than by using force or engaging in a power struggle. Toddlerhood is a stage during which games and diversions can be used to particularly good effect. When parents and caregivers make a game of what they want the toddler to do ("I'll bet I can beat you to the car!") or using creative ways of expressing their desires ("All the good girls in this house are going to put on their shoes so we can go and do something really exciting"), they are more likely to be successful.

CHAPTER 7

The School Years: Five to Twelve Years

With the increase in working mothers and single-parent families in the United States, day cares, nursery schools, and preschools have come to play a larger role in the care and education of children. But that change means that children go, almost literally, from being toddlers to being school-age children. Previously, the broad stage of childhood after toddlerhood was the preschool years. It is not so easy to identify such a stage any longer. Many children transition from the toddler years into the school years. However, it can still be said that the years between five and about twelve are the childhood years—the years when children discover the magic and excitement of play.

What to Expect During the School-Age Years

During the school-age stage of childhood, children develop enduring friendships. At the same time, they are embarking on an educational journey that will take them from preschool through elementary school on to middle school. But, more importantly, they learn the value of intense, same-sex friendships while they discover the magic of play.

Their play is greatly helped by the physical changes children in this period experience. While those physical changes are nowhere near as dramatic as what occurred during infancy and toddlerhood, the physical development of school-age children allows them to be engaged in sports and other kinds of physical activities.

At the same time, with their child's new reliance on peer relationships, parents become aware that their children are breaking away from them, becoming more self-sufficient and self-confident, and they are becoming more responsible and able to regulate both their behavior and their emotions. If there are still occasional emotional breakdowns, it is understandable with all the new stressors that occur at this stage of development.

Physical Development

The school-years stage is characterized by slow but steady physical growth. Children at this point in their development work on perfecting their motor abilities. During the school-age years, the average child gains between 2 and 2½ inches in height each year. Growth, though, tends to be concentrated in the area of their legs, arms, and faces. The weight gain during this period of growth is between 3 and 6 pounds per year. And by age eleven or twelve, all of their teeth have been replaced by permanent teeth and their brain growth is essentially complete.

During the school-age years, children's motor skills are refined and expanded. Through play and by analyzing the movements involved and by practicing motor skills endlessly, children between five and twelve are developing six basic motor behaviors:

- Running
- Jumping

- Sequencing foot movements
- Balancing
- Throwing
- Catching

This kind of motor activity is essential for the development of muscle tone, balance, coordination, strength, and endurance, and for stimulating body functions and improving metabolism.

As it turns out, most school-age children don't require lots of encouragement to participate in physical activity. They organize games, play on playground equipment, join sports teams, and are happily engaged in riding bikes, using skateboards, jumping rope, and skating. Unfortunately, there are children—some experts say more than 16 percent of American children— that simply are not developing in their arms, legs, and faces. Some are adding considerable weight and becoming obese.

ALERT

All parents are well aware of the benefits of having children play outside. According to one survey, the number of obese children has doubled during the last three decades. That tends to coincide with the rise in popularity of video games and the Internet. But it is not just the problem of carrying around too much weight that should concern parents. Children's cholesterol levels and blood pressure also have increased in recent years.

Children Need to Get Moving

The antidote to obesity is getting kids outside and involved in physical movement. Parents need to be aware of some of the strategies available for getting kids out of the house. Parents can help establish a schedule, so that they do not allow children to be involved in too many passive activities. Instead, a schedule may be designed to get them out of the house every day. It is also important for parents to get creative. By finding new and different ways to make outside fun truly enjoyable, parents can do such things as help children plan picnics, encourage them to romp with pets, plant a garden, or play games with friends.

Sports

Throughout the childhood years, children increasingly channel physical activity into constructive, goal-directed activities, such as sports. Part of the reason that kids get involved in sports is that they become more competitive and team sports become an outlet for the need to compete against others.

ALERT

Despite the many advantages of team sports, children can be hurt by playing sports, too. Sports-related physical injuries range from bumps and bruises to broken bones and serious concussions. Research shows that the risk of injury is greatest in football and least in soccer and swimming. Parents need to make sure children always wear the proper protective equipment.

According to the New York University Child Study Center, research shows that sports contribute to the psychological well-being of children by reducing anxiety and depression while enhancing self-esteem. Through sports children are able to have social contact with their peers, learn about the value of teamwork and cooperation, and engage in critical thinking while learning to solve problems. Also, the benefits of sports include the building of self-discipline, trust, respect for others, leadership, and coping skills. And, of course, sports help kids recognize the importance of physical fitness.

Cognitive Development

Children's thinking is gradually becoming more sophisticated as they mature; however, between the ages of about seven and twelve, their thought processes change dramatically. At around seven or eight children become capable of making logical decisions. They are able—often for the first time—to think more like adults. There is also more flexibility, logic, and objectivity in their thinking. They can look at situations from different points of views and perspectives, and that ability allows them to take the viewpoint of others. And, they can recognize there is more than one solution to a problem. Furthermore, their thinking has improved so that they understand time, speed, and distance much better. Finally, children of this age also have better short-term and long-term memory capacity.

Private Speech and Cognitive Development

Laura E. Berk, is one of the foremost authorities on what is called "private speech," which she has studied for more than twenty years. A distinguished professor of psychology at Illinois State University, Berk has discovered that private speech can account for 20 to 60 percent of the remarks a child younger than ten makes. Even though some parents regard this audible chatter as a sign of disobedience, inattentiveness, or even mental instability, Berk says that private speech is an essential part of cognitive development for all children.

Once children's cognitive operations become well practiced, they start to think words rather than saying them. Gradually, then, private speech gets internalized as silent, inner speech. Berk has found that when children have warm and responsive parents, those children used more self-guiding private speech. No matter what the task or the goal, children who used private speech appropriate for their age were the most successful.

QUESTION

Is it abnormal for my seven-year-old to talk aloud to himself?
Just like younger children, older children, even seven-year-olds, use what is called private speech. Child psychologists who have studied private speech say it is an essential part of cognitive development in children.

How do parents encourage children to develop private speech? According to Dr. Berk, private speech emerges out of rich, verbal, collaborative communication between a parent and a child. The parent adapts his or her communication to fit the child's developmental needs related to the task at hand, guiding, offering support, and suggesting effective strategies.

Furthermore, Berk says that verbal dialogue between a parent and child is the best way to promote task-oriented, self-regulating private speech. The major function of private speech, she says, is self-regulation.

Social and Emotional Development

There is a world of difference between the toddler and the school-age child in terms of emotional expression and emotional regulation during this period of childhood. Although self-regulation develops at each child's pace and likely proceeds gradually and unevenly, it is well established that children who cry, whine, hit, bite, or swear to get their way will not be well liked and will experience delays in their social development.

Emotionally, it is difficult for children to hold back their feelings until after about age three. However, after a child enters school, the developing sense of self will be strongly influenced by the relationships they have with other children. It is important to be aware that a child's relationship with other children increases to about six hours a day at school and up to three or four hours a day after school.

Given the influence of peers, as well as the continuing influence of parents and family, by about ages nine or ten the typical school-age child is at least able to give the general impression of being in control of her emotions. At this age a child may still get angry, particularly if she feels someone is being unfair. But her anger is less likely to become physical, as was the case in earlier years.

Self-Regulation

The goal of socialization of children is to help them achieve self-regulation—the ability to control their behavior on their own. Life for children is full of various temptations to veer away from the acceptable courses of action. But a child's ability to resist these temptations is a consequence of both his own emerging thinking capacities as well as the guidance of his parents, his siblings, and his other socializing agents, such as teachers.

In the early toddler stage, children are dependent, for the most part, on their parents and caregivers who administer various kinds of disciplinary practices to help increase their resistance to temptation. These practices often include punishment along with explanations of the need for compliance.

As the child develops, parents shift their control strategies from physical to verbal (using more explanations, bargaining, and verbal reprimands). These strategies aid the child's own abilities to use more verbally based control strategies. In the next phase the child gains the ability to comply with parental or adult expectations in the absence of external supervision.

As children mature, they not only learn to use self-control strategies more efficiently but they become more aware of which ones work best. Gradually they learn to use a range of techniques, including self-distraction, self-instruction, or redefinition of the object.

Researchers suggest that success in self-regulation comes about because of two basic factors: genetics and parenting. Some children are born with traits that are likely to help them have higher levels of self-regulation. For instance, a child with an easygoing temperament is likely to be better at self-regulating. Aside from genetics, though, studies have shown that parents can play an important role in helping their children develop higher levels of self-regulation.

For example, children exhibiting self-regulation are associated with parents who offer their children emotional support. To be emotionally supportive, parents must give meaningful praise to their child, be sensitive to her needs, and be encouraging. The opposite characteristics in parents—criticism, coldness, indifference to a child's needs, and harsh controls—are associated with poor self-regulation in children.

Cognitive Support and Structure

Cognitive support from parents is also important for the development of self-regulation. Cognitive support would include intellectual stimulation and providing intellectual resources in the home. Furthermore, there is evidence that children gain self-regulation skills when their parents encourage them to be autonomous and when they provide support for that autonomy.

Also, research suggests that children need the support that comes from a home environment featuring structure and consistent rules. When parents provide daily routines that make life predictable within the home and family, a child is better able to adjust his own behavior to conform to the routines.

When a child has to learn to modify his own desires and wishes to conform to the rules of your home, he is getting daily practice in self-regulation.

Making Friends

Socialization is in part about being self-regulated, but it might also be said to be about learning to play by the rules. And that's where peers help out. Peers offer a different perspective than the family does. Peers provide information about how to play by the rules of the social game and about how well a child plays. Research shows that peer reinforcement, what friends enjoy and reward versus what peers ignore or reject, affects the behavior patterns of children.

Furthermore, peers serve as models for each other. Children learn new social skills by imitating what other kids do. Children tend to imitate older, more powerful, and more prestigious peer models.

Children learn to play by the rules often by playing together. It's in games and play that children have most of their social interactions. Not only do they play together in school, but they spend more of their time outside of school playing with friends than they spend in any other activity.

What Is Play?

Play has been described as intrinsically motivated rather than imposed or directed by others; it is concerned with means, not ends; it is free from external rules; it is nonserious and highly engaging. Given this definition, play provides an environment in which children can discover the world without significant risk.

What happens in play? Children learn not only to make use of their own fantasies but also to act them out. They learn behaviors that are appropriate to each play situation. Without fear, they test the limits of what's acceptable. And, very importantly, they learn whether they are accepted by their peers. Few things are more important to children than acceptance by their peers. Getting along with friends and acquaintances is a child's first experience of interaction with the world at large.

Peer Relationship Milestones

The interactions with other children take on different forms as children grow and mature. Here are some significant milestones in children's peer relationships:

- Four-and-a-half years: Children begin to have longer play sessions and they are willing to accept roles other than that of the main character.
- Six years: They reach a peak in imaginative play.
- Seven years: Children begin to choose same-gender playmates.
- Eight to twelve years: The main goal of friendship is to be accepted by their same-gender peers.
- Nine to eleven years: Children expect friends to accept and admire them and to be loyal and committed to the relationship.
- Eleven to thirteen years: They expect genuineness, intimacy, self-disclosure, common interests, and similar attitudes and values in friends.

Common Problems of School-Age Children

Some of the common problems of school-age children include aggression, bullying, and shyness. How children express aggression as they mature from toddlers to school-age kids changes. In the toddler and preschool stages, they usually display aggression related to toys and possessions. This is called instrumental aggression. And in wanting a toy or a possession, children fight, frequently using physical means to obtain or keep a toy they want. As they move to ages six and seven, they are more likely to display hostile aggression, using criticism, ridicule, name-calling, and tattling. Between ages seven and twelve physical aggression declines and verbal aggression becomes much more common.

Bullying

Bullying is usually defined as repeated and systematic efforts to inflict harm on another person by means of physical attacks, verbal attacks, or social attacks. There are gender differences in bullying as boys are more likely to use physical aggression to attack a target, but girls are most likely to mock or ridicule their victims.

Once bullying was looked on as a normal part of the school-age child's life and play experience. But no longer is bullying viewed in this way. Bullying is a serious problem harming both the victim and the bully. Studies have shown that 10 to 17 percent of children may be bullied at one time or another. And middle school is the prime time for bullying, especially bullying related to sexual harassment.

QUESTION

Why does my son get picked on at school?
The evidence seems to suggest that one reason why some children are targeted by bullies is that they send out signals that they are unlikely to defend themselves or are unwilling to retaliate. In other words, they seem to let others know they are likely victims.

Children who are less likely to be the victims of bullies are those who have friends. Not only is it important to have friends, but the type of friends makes a difference as well. A child who has friends with physical strength and who are somewhat aggressive themselves offer protection for children against bullying and aggression.

ALERT

Children who are bullied are often anxious, depressed, and underachieving. And when former victims are studied many years later, they tend to suffer from lower self-esteem.

Helping Children Cope with Bullies

Experts recognize these days that bullying is a social problem in schools and that efforts to stop bullying must involve changes to the social climate. Educating the school staff, as well as all students, to the dangers of bullying is often an important first step. Schools also must redesign aspects of school life so that there is adequate adult supervision at all times so bullying cannot easily take place. In addition, counselors must be available to see to it that both victims and bullies get help. Victims need help to learn how not to be targets. Bullies need help to learn how to interact with others without aggression.

Parents can play a valuable role in helping their child cope with bullying. They can teach their child to make friends so that the child is rarely if ever isolated or alone at school. Furthermore, bullies often pick on children who won't stand up for themselves or retaliate. Teaching a child to be more assertive and to stand up to bullies is very important in reducing the victimization that might occur at school.

Shyness

Shyness means a child has social anxiety and inhibited social behavior. Some children seem to be born with a temperament that makes them more withdrawn and less outgoing. However, child psychologists who have studied shyness find that children can be helped to overcome some of their shy and timid behavior so that temperament does not become their destiny.

There are a variety of strategies that have been developed to help shy children become more socially outgoing. Those strategies involve coaching them to practice more outgoing behaviors, modeling more assertive and out-going behaviors, and following daily instructions for actually doing non-shy things at school with peers and even teachers.

Changing Relationships with Parents

During later childhood when children are refining their cognitive and social skills they are also becoming more self-directed while at the same time they are choosing more of how they spend their time. From ages five to twelve, their friendships are expanding and their peer relationships seem—at times—more important than their relationships with their parents.

However, the growing importance of friendships does not lessen the importance of parents in their lives. The family and parental influence remains strong during these years. For instance, as the thinking and emotions of children show greater maturity, their parents often give young people more responsibility, particularly in terms of household chores.

Also, parents change their discipline and parenting approaches so that they are more apt to use reasoning to get their kids to adhere to rules and limits. There is also more concern, on the child's part, at least, with equality and fairness in the parent-child relationship. Therefore, parents are also more likely to do more monitoring and less directing of their child. As part of their cognitive growth, school-age children have a greater understanding of the legitimacy of their parent's authority over them. Kids become more appreciative of the fact that their parents are more experienced than they are and that their parents may be making decisions for their own good.

Anger as Part of the Parent-Child Relationship

All parents love the warm fuzzy moments with their children, especially those times when their child gives out a big hug and says, "Mommy, I really love you!" Or the child snuggles up to his father and says, "You're the best daddy in the world!" However, it isn't so warm and fuzzy when your child, in an angry tantrum yells, "I hate you!" or "I wish you were dead!"

Although some children will utter such things at age three or four, most often parents are likely to hear this when their child is between the ages of seven and ten. The reason is related in part to the fact that parents have to put limits on their growing child during these years. They have to say "no" more often as their child gets older and wants more privileges and freedom. But placing limits on a child's activities and telling them no once in a while is not going to make parents popular.

Parents should be prepared and expect, if they are doing a competent job as parents placing limits and restating rules, that they will at times make their child furious, and in his fury, the child will say rash things—such as, "I hate you!"

It is important for parents to keep calm and acknowledge what their child is feeling. If parents are too personally invested in hearing only the warm and gooey comments from their child, they may well feel devastated when they get "I wish you weren't my mother" or "I'm going to run away from home to get away from you!"

However, parents need to be well-balanced enough and confident enough in their decisions so they can respond with, "I know you're very angry with me right now and you don't like me." Then parents should give a rationale as to why they denied their child something the child felt was important. By giving a reasonable explanation, they are letting their child know that they didn't make an arbitrary and capricious decision.

Moral Development

As children spend more extensive time with their peers, the way they think about moral rules changes. Their thinking becomes more complicated. While some children develop rather rigid rules and ways of thinking about what is right and wrong, others have a much less rigid and somewhat looser approach.

Moral development refers to the process by which children adopt principles that lead them to decide what is right behavior and what is wrong behavior. There are, however, various theories about the stages of moral development in children. No one theory has been universally accepted. And it seems quite clear that some children who talk about what they believe related to moral behavior, may not actually act in a moral way in certain situations.

Child psychologists today often discuss prosocial behaviors. Prosocial behavior refers to ways of responding to other people that is sympathetic, helpful, comforting, cooperative, and altruistic. Research suggests that warm, affectionate parenting is essential for children to develop helping and altruistic behaviors, although parental anger and punishment is generally not effective in bringing about prosocial behavior. By linking a child's behavior to the outcome for the victim ("Melissa is crying because you hit her") or giving reasons for another person's distress ("I'm upset because you are talking rudely to me") helps children to learn to be sympathetic and empathetic toward others.

CHAPTER 8

Adolescence:
The Teenage Stage

Adolescence is an exciting stage of development in which teens go from children to adults. Their bodies and minds are changing rapidly during the adolescent years while they are advancing in terms of social relationships, determining who they are, and developing altered relationships with their parents. At the end of the adolescent period, most teens will be ready to go on to the initial stages of adulthood with a clearer sense of who they are and how they fit into the world. However, in the process of going from child to adult, there are many possible pitfalls. These include peer pressure and risky behaviors. Many young teens are vulnerable to the seductions of alcohol, drugs, and cigarettes. While peer pressure may play a role in terms of teenagers choosing risky and dangerous behaviors, most adolescents still value the strength, support, and opinions of their parents.

Changing Bodies

Sometime between ages nine and sixteen, a child's body begins to change. These new and remarkable changes are all due to puberty. There are biological reasons for these changes. When a child's body reaches a certain stage of growth, a part of the brain called the pituitary gland signals the sex glands—the ovaries for girls and the testicles for boys—to start working. The ovaries and the testicles then signal other parts of the body, telling them to start to grow. These signals are carried throughout the body by **hormones**, the male hormone testosterone and the female hormones estrogen and progesterone.

The hormones cause most of the bodily changes that occur during and after puberty: the growth of body hair, the development of breasts, the deepening of voices, and menstruation. In addition, bodily proportions change as well. And both boys and girls develop muscle.

The adolescent growth spurt lasts about four or four-and-a-half years. For boys, peak growth occurs at around age thirteen; for girls it is about age eleven. As parents of teens can attest, the nutritional needs of teenagers increase considerably during this growth spurt, with teenagers ingesting generous amounts of food and beverage.

All of these changes are related to becoming an adult and getting ready to be able to become mothers and fathers. Of course, the physical changes don't really mean adolescents are emotionally or psychologically prepared to take on the adult responsibilities of being parents, but physically, by early adolescence, they are ready to produce babies. However, there is greater significance to their bodily changes. Both boys and girls grow taller and more muscular. This makes them more prepared for sports and physical activities.

Growing Minds

While a teenager's body is developing rapidly, his mind is changing so that he is able to accomplish intellectual tasks more easily, more quickly, and more efficiently than possible at younger ages.

This advanced thinking prowess makes it possible for teenagers to use sophisticated strategies to aid their memories, for example. And they are capable of using a future time perspective, something they couldn't do at younger ages. They have an awareness that much of life consists of anticipating, formulating, and developing strategies for solving problems.

Teens are able to deal with increasingly complex educational and vocational demands. This makes it possible for adolescents to take classes in geometry, physics, and calculus, as well as to successfully write essays about the metaphors in poetry in English classes.

Along with other cognitive changes, teenagers are able to entertain hypotheses or theoretical propositions. This new ability helps them look critically at both ideas and people. Unfortunately for parents, these new-found cognitive skills lead teens to view their parents in new ways, often finding fault with them or exposing their faults or inconsistencies.

A Teen's Brain Is a Work in Progress

Just because teens act like adults, doesn't mean they are adults, nor does it mean that they should be dealt with like an adult. Teenagers usually do know right from wrong and they are usually smart enough and mature enough to know what they should do; yet often they fail to act in an appropriately responsible manner.

Consequently, adolescents will race cars, impulsively shoplift, carry a weapon to school for protection, or try to outrun a speeding train at a crossing. Many would argue that they deserve whatever happens to them. Others aren't so sure.

For instance, scientists studying the brain development of adolescents have found in recent years that the brain is not fully developed during childhood or early adolescence. In fact, significant brain development continues throughout the teen years and into the twenties. And researchers at the University of California Los Angeles have discovered that the frontal lobe, the area of the brain most responsible for judgment and self-control, undergoes far more changes during adolescence than at any other stage of life. The frontal lobe is also, researchers have learned, the last part of the brain to develop.

What this slow development of the frontal lobe means is that even though adolescents are fully capable in many areas, they cannot reason as well as adults. Dr. Jay Giedd, a researcher at the National Institute of Mental Health, explains that the frontal lobe, which helps people organize, plan, and strategize, is not fully developed until sometime after many individuals are well into their twenties. Giedd says it's unfair to expect teenagers to have adult levels of organizational skills or decision-making skills before their brains are fully developed.

ESSENTIAL

Part of the cognitive changes experienced by adolescents is a preoccupation with thought itself. They are at times obsessed with their own thoughts. This leads them to be too introspective and analytical, not to mention egocentric. In other words, they think about themselves a lot. In their minds, they are thinking that if they themselves are thinking about themselves so much, then other people may be thinking about them just as much. This, then, is why teens become so much more self-conscious.

Do Teenagers Have to Rebel?

For more than a century and a half, teenagers have been characterized by the stereotype of the rebellious teen who is against his parents and conventional society in general. The stereotype includes the long-haired hippy teen or the violent, skinhead adolescent. Or the teenaged gang member who participates in drug use and gratuitous violence. Or the tattooed teenager with various forms of jewelry sticking out of various parts of her anatomy.

QUESTION

My teenager thinks I don't allow her enough freedom. Is this common? It is very common. One of the aspects of the teen years is growing independence and a wish for fewer restrictions. Parents are better off recognizing this and gradually allowing more freedom and greater responsibility while being ready to rein in the leash if teenagers prove they can't handle the freedom they say they want.

But are these teens the norm or are they *atypical* teenagers who give the rest of the adolescent population a bad reputation? The fact is that only a minority of teenagers rebel against their parents or society at large. Most adolescents have a relatively smooth teenage period, and while they may not always see eye-to-eye with their parents and other adults, they are not intent on making life miserable for all adults.

Adolescents and Risky Behavior

Teenagers engage in various risky behaviors. Such risky behaviors might include playing extreme sports, trying drugs, engaging in unprotected sex, or indulging in binge drinking. The Harvard School of Public Health estimates that 44 percent of college students—many of whom are still adolescents— regularly binge drink. A study published in the *Journal of American College Health* indicates that frequent binge drinkers were eight times more likely to miss classes, fall behind in schoolwork, or damage property.

ESSENTIAL

Some psychologists have argued that risk taking and experimentation by adolescents serves developmentally appropriate functions. For example, it can facilitate peer interaction, teach youth how to deal with behaviors that might be illegal when older, and help in their **identity** achievement. In other words, risks can be opportunities that help them to develop into healthy adults.

Teenagers are notorious risk takers—not all of them, of course, but a good many. But risk-taking is not necessarily a bad thing for teenagers. In fact, some risk-taking may be important to adolescent development. It seems almost inevitable that every adolescent will take risks at some times. Whether a teen experiments with smoking, drinking, rebelling against the curfew his parents set for him, or refusing to wear a helmet when he's riding his bicycle, risk-taking is certain to show up sooner or later.

But these kinds of risks may be ways of asserting independence or even satisfying a teen's curiosity. In a sense, this kind of risk-taking is somewhat like sticking a toe in the lake before going for a swim. Test it out, see how it feels, and then take the big plunge.

Obviously, no parent wants his teenager to experience lifelong consequences for mistakes or for trying things out. However, in a sense, without risks there might not be sufficient growth for teens. Try to regulate your teenager's life too closely and you might be able to keep her from taking any risks and you thereby eliminate the possibility of her ever getting hurt. However, keep a repressive thumb on her too heavily, or for too long, and you run the risk of creating a young person who is afraid to ever try anything that is a bit risky.

For parents, though, it is always important to consider a teen's risky behaviors in the broader context of her life. Is her risky behavior one that she and her group of generally high-achieving and positively motivated friends decided to try or is her risky behavior part of a pattern of negative or dangerous behavior? Answer that question and you may decide to ignore some risky behaviors or you may decide that she needs intervention or treatment.

Teens and Substance Abuse

Each year, in order to learn more about drug, alcohol, and tobacco use by young people, the Institute for Social Research at the University of Michigan conducts and reports on a national study of youth in grades eight, ten, and twelve. Published annually as the *Monitoring the Future* surveys, the statistics are widely respected as providing some of the best information on current trends among our youth in terms of their use of illicit drugs as well as alcohol.

FACT

Findings from the NIAAA indicate that, of those individuals who began drinking before age fourteen, 47 percent experienced alcohol problems at some future point, while only 9 percent of people who started drinking after age twenty-one became dependent on alcohol.

Recent statistics from the *Monitoring the Future* survey shows that 15 percent of eighth-grade students reported they had drunk alcohol in the past thirty days. And that number nearly triples (44 percent) for students in grade twelve.

The significance of these numbers is related to what the National Institute on Alcohol Abuse and Alcoholism (NIAAA) has reported about early alcohol use. Based on research with a random sample of 43,000 U.S. adults, the NIAAA found that those people who began drinking in their early teens were at greater risk of developing alcohol problems in later life.

It's no secret that teenagers are not adults and that they have considerable developing to do in regard to their bodies, their emotions, and their brains. It is not surprising, therefore, that the NIAAA also discovered that early drinkers were at the greatest risk of developing alcohol dependence more quickly and at younger ages. Young drinkers were the most likely to develop chronic, relapsing dependency on alcohol.

Even when other factors—such as a family history of alcoholism, depression, and childhood antisocial behavior—were controlled in studies, early drinking seemed to be one of the most critical elements in later diagnoses of alcohol dependence or abuse.

QUESTION

Would it be better if I allowed my adolescent to drink at home where I could supervise her?
A recent study reported in the *Journal of Studies on Alcohol and Drugs* found that teenagers who are allowed to drink alcohol at home tend to drink more outside the home than their peers who were not allowed to drink at home. Some parents believe that if they allow their children to try alcohol at home, this will not only teach them how to drink in a controlled setting, but it will also remove the "forbidden fruit" temptation that many teens might experience. This particular study from the *Journal of Studies on Alcohol and Drugs* seems to belie this popular notion.

What Parents Can Do

Rather than just be alarmed or frightened by the statistics, parents can take steps to reduce the risk of their child or teen beginning to use drugs or alcohol. In his *How to Raise a Drug-Free Kid: The Straight Dope for Parents*, Joseph A. Califano, the founder and chairman of The National Center on Addiction and Substance Abuse (CASA) at Columbia University, and the former U.S. Secretary of Health, Education, and Welfare, presents suggestions for parents to take to cut down on their child's risk of using drugs.

ALERT

A recent report from CASA centers on the importance of family dinners. The report makes it very clear that when teenagers eat dinner fewer than three times a week with their families they are twice as likely to use tobacco or marijuana, one and a half times as likely to use alcohol, and twice as likely to use drugs in the future. The research comparing teens who use alcohol and drugs with those who do not use alcohol and drugs found that a critical factor is the frequency of family dinners.

One of the significant recommendations Califano makes in his book is that parents must be engaged in their child's life. Children of engaged parents, Califano points out, are far less likely to smoke, drink, or use other drugs. And how do you become an engaged parent? Califano lists nine facets of parental engagement:

1. Get involved in your child's life and activities.
2. Open the lines of communication and keep them open.
3. Be a good role model: Your actions are more persuasive than your words.
4. Set rules and expect your children to follow them.
5. Monitor your child's whereabouts.
6. Maintain family rituals such as eating dinner together.
7. Incorporate religious and spiritual practices into your family life.
8. Get Dad engaged—and keep him engaged.
9. Engage the larger family of your children's friends, teachers, classmates, neighbors, and community.

Friendships and Self-Discovery

A trend that started with the early school-age child continues into adolescence. That is, peer relationships develop and become more and more important as children get older. In adolescence, however, relationships with friends grow deeper because adolescents need both self-understanding and identity achievement. And what happens is that, in friendships during the teen years, adolescents discover more about their inner feelings as well as what they think and believe, which by and large happens through relationships.

Peer group membership is also an important part of identity because the group of friends a teen has helps to define who and what he is. Peer groups, whether they are referred to as **cliques**, crowds, or "the gang," offer opportunities to try on different roles, and this is an important part of identity formation.

Teenagers want to share their inner feelings. This intense desire for self-disclosure results in long hours of talking to friends. These conversations, which parents often think are excessive, are important for expressing who they are, what they think, and what they believe.

Although friendships in the late school-age years and in early adolescence are usually rather transitory and fleeting, by the late teen years, young people have the ability to maintain stable relationships.

FACT

By age sixteen, 90 percent of teens are dating. Often it is in mid-adolescence, around ages fourteen to sixteen, that sexual experimentation takes place. While both dating and sexuality may coincide, most middle teenagers are not really capable of emotional intimacy.

The Influence of Peers

At the same time that teens are becoming more autonomous and less dependent on their parents, they are turning toward their peers and becoming more dependent on them. However, it is mostly in the early teen years, around twelve and thirteen, that there is the greatest conformity to the peer group's beliefs and behavior. But when parents see this happening, they begin to fear that their influence and authority with their child is waning. While that is true to some extent, it doesn't mean teens are really rejecting basic values they learned at home.

In fact, peer influence does not replace parental influence except in some areas. On the superficial level—in terms of clothes, hair styles, and music preference, for instance—teens look to their peers for guidance. Parents remain highly influential when it comes to the really important aspects of a teen's life: values, future goals, and philosophy of life.

Peer Pressure

The concept of peer pressure gets a bad reputation. Actually, it is an overrated concept that gets blamed when teens make mistakes. The fact is that peer pressure is not always bad and that it works as much in a positive direction as it does in a negative one. It all depends on which crowd or group a teen hangs around with. Hang around with the jocks and he will be influenced to be involved in sports. Hang around with the academically oriented and she will be influenced to get good grades. Hang around with drug users and, yes, he will likely be influenced to use drugs.

Another myth is that peers will always lead teens astray. This tends to suggest that adolescents are passive and are easily influenced by any teenager or group that comes along. But this idea is a misconception. What is more likely to be true is that teens choose friends who have the same values and attitudes as they have. Adolescents tend to gravitate to those other teens who have the same problems or the same view of the world. In effect, then, teens tend to find others like themselves and then they do things that they all were thinking of doing anyway.

Figuring Out Who They Are

People often say that the greatest task of middle adolescence is to answer the Big Question. That Big Question is: Who am I?

Erik Erikson, who developed the stages of psychosocial development, has viewed adolescence as a struggle to find an identity. Erikson suggests that the search for an identity is such a struggle because adolescents are undergoing rapid physical changes and at the same having to face various adult tasks and decisions. The great task for teens is to deal with a variety of new roles—as friend, student, athlete, employee, boyfriend or girlfriend, for instance—in order to come to terms with themselves and their environment.

But this task is not easy. There is much ambiguity and uncertainty in an adolescent's life and world, and there is a tendency for many teens to overcommit themselves to cliques or gangs, allegiances, loves, activities, and even social causes. And, at times, they have no idea who they are.

But after trying on different roles on this journey to self-identity, most teens figure out who they are. Most achieve inner stability that corresponds to what others perceive them to be. When an adolescent feels comfortable with who he is and feels confidence about the person he thinks he is, he has solved the identity crisis. And he has answered the Big Question with a more confident: This is who I am.

What Teens Need from Their Parents

Often teens may say that they don't want their parents in their lives. And they may try to make it clear to their mothers and fathers that they can take care of themselves and they don't need the interference of repressive parents. But they are just being impulsive, overconfident, and a bit premature about their ability to function in their world without the backup of their families.

ESSENTIAL

In most healthy families, values are advocated from an early age. Typically, parents have modeled morality, while helping their child develop a sense of what is right and wrong, good and bad. In addition, most parents have talked about what they believe is right and wrong, and by doing this have passed valuable information to their child that will help guide her in making decisions when no parent is present. Psychologists usually characterize this development as moral reasoning.

Most teenagers still need their parents' support, guidance, and limit-setting. They very much need a stable anchor in their sea of uncertainty. That stability should come from their parents who present a consistent home life that features stability, a basic value system, religious education, and the comfort of unconditional love and acceptance.

Of course, parents need to be letting go of their teen and giving them more freedom and greater responsibility. But at the same time, there has to be a balance between freedom and the limits and rules that should be set to help compensate for the lack of total adult development in the area of reasoning, judgment, and decision-making.

Coping with Their Growing Independence

Throughout childhood and adolescence people are changing. But, as it turns out, so are parents. As teens demand more independence, freedom, and autonomy, parents must continually adapt to these demands. Of course, it doesn't mean that parents throw up their hands in despair and passive surrender. It simply means that parents recognize that kids are changing and that parents must shift in their role from one of authority to one permitting their growing child to develop her own individuality. That is a balancing act, though, in which parents still provide what adolescents need—security, support, supervision, and limits—while allowing them enough freedom to try out their individuality and learn to be responsible.

CHAPTER 9

Raising Successful Kids

When should parents start being concerned about raising a successful child? Some would argue that it is right after conception; others might say it is at the moment of birth. Either way, most agree that concern and efforts to raise a successful child should start early. There are any number of things that parents can do to promote the successful development of children. Those include providing adequate nutrition, establishing a solid attachment relationship, teaching socialization skills, providing appropriate discipline, and promoting education. A number of strategies, tactics, and approaches will be discussed below that can guide parents in making sure their child is raised successfully.

Forming Early Attachments

Attachment is the strong bond that develops between an infant and her caregiver. Without this bond between parent and child, it may not be possible for an infant to survive and flourish. Without a proper attachment between the young child and one or both parents, the child's emotional, physical, social, psychological health and well-being suffer damaging consequences.

How do parents facilitate a **securely attached infant**? They do so through various skills, tactics, and parenting behaviors that include:

- Smiling at the child
- Gently handling the infant
- Stroking the child
- Feeding the baby
- Talking to the infant

In general, though, the most vital action in bringing about a strong attachment is to be responsive to the child's needs. By providing love, affection, gentle handling, and responsiveness to the baby's needs, that child comes to feel loved and he comes to establish a basic trust in people and the environment. With this basic trust, a young child will feel secure exploring the environment and doing so with a sense of curiosity. This curiosity helps promote mental and social growth.

Children who have successfully formed an attachment during infancy have the ability to:

1. Satisfactorily deal with novel situations
2. Cope with failure
3. Exert perseverance in problem solving
4. Participate in loving relationships with others
5. Maintain a healthy self-esteem

These skills and abilities are the result of a strong, positive attachment.

Supervise and Monitor

Beginning during the toddler years, children desire to take on greater responsibility. For instance, toddlers want to dress themselves or feed themselves. Later, at about age five, children want to try things—like carrying groceries, riding a bicycle in a busy street, or using a knife to cut a box—that their parents may judge are not safe.

As children are growing and developing during the first five years and beyond, the wise parent is encouraging autonomy and independence. At the same time, they are ever alert to situations or activities that involve too much responsibility. This could mean that a parent may allow certain activities only under strict supervision or in a practice situation. However, it is often in such controlled situations that parents hear the typical lament, "But why can't I do it? Everyone else gets to do it!"

Anytime a child shows that she has been allowed—or has taken on her own—too much responsibility, parents need to check up on her and monitor her activities. Even during, maybe one should say, *particularly* during adolescence, young people need supervision and monitoring. While teens may feel like they are already adults, research shows otherwise.

FACT

There is evidence that inconsistent supervision of youth by their parents can promote behavior problems or delinquency. More recent data show that youths who believe their parents care little about their activities are more likely to engage in illegal activities than those who believe their actions will be closely monitored.

That's why it's important for parents to continue to provide close supervision. And along with supervision and monitoring, parents often have to place limits on teens by saying "No." Doing this may bring a howl of protest from an adolescent who believes he is being unfairly restricted or repressed, but parents who place limits on their teens while also exercising close supervision are likely to help their child stay out of serious difficulty.

Set Limits and Rules

When I was talking to the parent of a middle school student recently, the mother said she didn't always understand her daughter.

"We know kids need limits and in fact the experts say that kids seem to thrive when they have limits," she said. "Furthermore, kids often seem to want rules, right?"

I shook my head in agreement. I knew there was more she had to say.

"So, if this is true," she continued, "why do they get so angry and upset when we impose rules and limits?"

"Good question," I answered. "Just because almost everyone, including kids, knows he needs limits, doesn't mean that children and teens always like the limits we set for them. Nor does it mean that they have enough insight to really know that limits are important for their healthy development."

Then, I had a discussion with a high school teacher. "I had this guy in my class," the teacher said, "and he wouldn't stop playing with his cell phone when I was trying to teach some new concepts. So, I stopped the lecture and told him I would like it if he put his phone away so we could do our lesson."

But the teenager's response was instant and visceral. "You can't take my phone away from me!" the boy said. "You're not my mother and you can't touch me either."

The teacher remained calm and responded in a quiet, but firm voice, "I'll wait until the phone is put away and you're ready to go on with our work."

This didn't quite placate the young man either. "I'll hit you if you touch me," he said in an aggressive tone.

"I'll wait for you to do what you need to do," the teacher said. She waited and eventually the kid put his cell phone away and the lesson resumed.

"I think this boy doesn't have a lot of limits set for him," the teacher said. "He seems to be used to getting his own way. I suspect that when he gets angry, people back off and let him do what he wants. Nobody seems willing to set normal limits for him, or they try to do it with threats of physical intervention, but it's clear he needs limits."

I agreed with the teacher. And I told her about a teenage girl in one of my juvenile court groups. This girl is fifteen and has remarked that she has few rules at home and if she comes home late her parents won't be waiting up for her and they aren't there to confront her about the lateness of her coming home.

"My mother is like my best friend," the girl has said. "She lets me do whatever I want."

I, of course, did not say this to her, but to myself I thought: "And that, young lady, is why you are on probation to the juvenile court."

This girl, we can call her Lisa, has very poor self-control, is frequently aggressive with her peers, and enjoys baiting adults to watch their reactions. Lisa is a teen who has needed firm limits and rules for a long time. Unfortunately, it took her getting into serious trouble to get placed on probation and to begin to receive limits imposed by a juvenile court.

It's nice to have a positive relationship with your child. But you are not your child's best friend. You're her parent. And that means that when you set limits and rules you might not win a popularity contest—at least not that day.

In order for children to learn to set limits on themselves they need parents to place limits on them throughout childhood and adolescence. And, of course, it won't mean they will appreciate your doing this. But that's okay. They don't have to thank you for telling them no and putting restrictions on what they can do.

You can take a measure of comfort and satisfaction later when they're adults and they have well-balanced lives that include their ability to delay gratification and place limits on themselves. They might not even know how they got so good at making choices in their lives—but you'll know.

Fostering Independence and Autonomy

The process of becoming independent and autonomous begins in the toddler years. However, it shifts into full throttle when kids become teenagers. The developmental task of becoming their own persons and separating from their parents may be one of the most stressful developmental tasks of all. One of the reasons for this is that while adolescents want to be psychologically free from their parents, they still desire to keep the secure, dependent relationship of early and middle childhood.

It is not unusual for a middle teenager to want to share secrets with a mom or a dad one day, and the next day harshly criticize the parent for trying to keep him a baby. That's one of the great conflicts of adolescence: trying to be both dependent and independent at the same time.

Parents should try to foster their teenager's independence and autonomy, but often there is such a hostile atmosphere that parents are not sure what else they can do to help their child achieve greater freedom. Perhaps the biggest thing a parent can do is to try to treat their teen with respect while at the same time allowing him to vacillate between the need for dependence and independence. If a parent can recognize that it is a stressful task for an adolescent to detach himself from the family, the parent can be more appreciative of why the teenager may be so inconsistent, hostile, and withdrawn.

Hold Them Close

There are many aspects of parenting that indicate love. One such element of parenting is offering security and protection. Perhaps holding children close is a way of showing love, support, and protection. However, the phrase "hold them close" can have multiple meanings. For instance, in early childhood, it might mean, very correctly, that sometimes children have to be held tightly and firmly.

ESSENTIAL

Letting go means giving children and teens more responsibility, demanding more from them, allowing them to try things on their own (which involves their making mistakes along the way), and granting increasing independence as parents trust them more.

Holding a young child firmly is a way of giving support to stop a child from continuing a behavior she is incapable of stopping on her own. Holding firmly and closely involves physically restraining a child with a gentle, but firm grip. It can come in handy with a young child who is out of control and posing a danger to himself and others. Young children who have not yet mastered their impulses may act wild and appear unable to put limits on themselves or refrain from breaking household rules—or indeed household objects. A big, long bear hug, in which you wrap yourself literally around your child, can be effective with angry, out-of-control kids. If a parent adds soothing talk, it may help a child calm himself.

But "hold them close" has another meaning. It means letting go of our child. In the early years you must hold children close, develop a secure relationship with them, make sure they feel loved, and give them plenty of warmth and protection. Then, having accomplished a secure relationship with them and protected them against whatever might harm them, parents must gradually let go.

Ultimately, parents must help children to grow up to be independent and self-sufficient. In order for children to be healthy and well-functioning adults, they have to be able to live on their own and support themselves. Discipline and childrearing tactics should always be based on this goal.

Parenting and Positive Self-Esteem

It's during middle childhood that a child develops positive—or negative—feelings about herself. Experts refer to these feelings as self-esteem and consider it to be a critical index of mental health. High self-esteem links to better life satisfaction and to happiness. Low self-esteem relates to depression, anxiety, and problems in school and in social relationships.

In some research self-esteem is closely related to patterns of childrearing. For example, some studies have found that parents of boys with high self-esteem used a style of parenting called authoritative. In this style, parents use firm control, promote high standards of behavior, encourage independence, and use reasoning with their children.

Other research suggests that children with high self-esteem have parents who are very accepting of their children, clearly define limits, and respect them for their individuality.

The Keys to Self-Discipline and Self-Control

It is during middle childhood that children learn about structure. Structure refers to those experiences that teach children to become self-disciplined in ways that rely more on positive self-esteem and much less on fear and shame. In order to teach children about structure parents have to shift their childrearing techniques—from methods that are calculated to provide physical care to those that are more concerned with psychological care and development.

Since there has been a shift in the child's world and the child goes from one of being dependent on parents to one in which there is greater interaction with peers, parents must recognize this in providing discipline and guidance. In effect, parents must realize that a school-age child's central world is often one of confrontation with peers in a competitive environment. Therefore, the discipline parents use in the middle childhood years should be aimed at assisting their children achieve social relationships that allow them to deal effectively with this competitive social atmosphere.

The guidance parents employ, then, is more related to reassuring their child, helping her bounce back from social mistakes or problems, and providing positive reinforcement for acquiring new skills, especially new social skills.

Supporting Cognitive Growth

In general, parents can support cognitive growth beginning at birth by providing a stimulating environment. This means that the home is a rich environment for the child that features a language, affection, attention, and learning.

In order that children know how to use language appropriately when they enter school and develop more extensive relationships with peers, they have to grow up in a home in which there is considerable language. Studies show that the more a mother talks to a child during the first year, the larger the child's vocabulary at seventeen months of age. But research goes beyond this to show that the more language spoken by adults (and siblings) in front of a child, the richer and more extensive the child's vocabulary throughout the preschool years.

Language acquisition is related to the development of other cognitive skills. The thought processes of a toddler are developing at the same time as language is developing. It is not exactly known that one skill causes the other to develop; rather, it is likely that each influences the other. Children need language to think and they need thought to have something to say.

Learning and IQ

Children will be at a disadvantage in school if they have low intellectual functioning. How a child succeeds at school is directly related to his **IQ** or his **intelligence**. Intelligence can be defined as the way children are measured on a standard intelligence test.

Those children who do poorly on IQ tests, and thus generally do less than average work at school, are those whose homes lack an intellectually stimulating environment. That would mean that there is less exposure to language, less exposure to books, and less exposure to opportunities to exercise their memories than the homes of children who do better.

Children with higher IQs generally have parents who:

- Are involved with them
- Are affectionate
- Are verbally responsive
- Avoid restrictions and punishment
- Provide a household that is organized
- Provide appropriate play materials
- Have predictable routines

It is well known that children who come to school prepared to learn are those children who have been exposed to language, reading, and other intellectual stimulation at home.

FACT

Studies have shown that those children who excel at school in the early years have been in homes in which there are many books. In fact, some research has shown that 500 or more books in the home relates to doing well at school.

Not only must there be books in the home, but parents need to be reading those books every day to their children. And even beyond just reading to them, parents must stimulate them intellectually by asking questions, and engaging in elementary forms of critical thinking while reading to them.

Encouraging Sex-Role Identity

Sex is not a role so much as it is an attribute that shapes many social roles. Sexual identity may, as well, influence the choice of future work and social relationships. In childhood and adolescence, sex-role identity will have an impact on friendships.

In early childhood children look to their same-sex parents to figure out the appropriate roles for males and females. However, aside from this observation, there are various theories in child psychology and child development to explain how boys learn to be boys and how girls learn to be girls. The social learning theory, for example, says that children learn through observation. According to this view, children observe that males and females act differently. Furthermore, this theory says that children learn that boys and girls are rewarded differently by adults for different kinds of behavior. Thus, they choose to engage in sex-appropriate behaviors that lead to approval or rewards from their parents.

ESSENTIAL

Children ages fourteen to twenty-two months show sexual differences in what they choose to play with. Boys are more likely to play with trucks and cars. Girls are more likely to play with dolls and soft toys. While most children seem to gravitate to toys generally preferred by boys or girls, there are some children who prefer toys usually favored by the opposite sex. This does not necessarily suggest that a child has a sexual identity problem.

Yet, despite various theories about how children acquire sex-role identity, there is considerable evidence that from a young age there are differences in the ways boys and girls behave. Not only do boys and girls play differently from the earliest ages, but what they choose to play with is different.

Regardless of the theories and what the experts say about how sex roles develop, and despite whatever bias parents have about not allowing their children to be stereotyped in terms of the toys they play with, it appears that parents, perhaps, have little to do with the sexual identities children develop. By age three, most children develop an identity as a boy or a girl. By age five or six, children know whether they are members of the male sex or the female sex.

CHAPTER 10

Families

The family has undergone dramatic changes in the United States in the last several decades. Fewer families are traditional families and there are fewer extended families to offer support and respite for children. There are more grandparents and other relatives raising children. There are more single parents raising children, and there is a significant number of families in which there are homosexual parents. Despite stresses within families, children can cope with changes and different kinds of family systems. If parents can shield their children from the stresses and turmoil that afflict far too many families, then the children have an opportunity to grow up healthy and happy.

The American Family Today

Maybe one time in the past we could characterize the traditional American family as a European Caucasian father who was the breadwinner; he was married to a European Caucasian woman who stayed at home and raised the children while caring for the household. But that kind of family is a relic of the past, if indeed there were such families aside from the late 1940s and the 1950s.

Today we have families where women play a much greater role in supporting the family. In fact, about three-quarters of all mothers of school-age children are employed. That's up from 50 percent in 1970 and 40 percent in 1960. Furthermore, fathers are spending more time with their children during the workweek today than they did just twenty years ago.

The family makeup, too, has undergone a radical change. There are about seventy million children under the age of seventeen in the United States and they live in these kinds of families:

- 70 percent of kids live with two parents.
- 26 percent of kids live with one parent.
- 4 percent live in households without any parent.
- Of the 4 percent who live with no parent, 50 percent live with grandparents, 19 percent live with other relatives, 25 percent live with nonrelatives, and some 300,000 live in foster homes.

FACT

Today there are about twelve million children receiving some form of child care on a regular basis from persons other than their parents. About three-and-a-half million children under the age of thirteen spend some time at home alone each week while their parents are at work.

Gay and Lesbian Parents

Along with a great variety of other parenting arrangements and amid the great diversity in families are gay and lesbian parents. A considerable number of homosexual men and women form families that may include children. Also, today there are more long-term and enduring relationships among homosexuals; research indicates that there are few differences between homosexual and heterosexual couples.

The presence of children in a homosexual relationship is more likely to exist where the couple is lesbian. Perhaps the reason for this is that women generally are awarded custody of children following a divorce, so the children may go with a mother who is in a lesbian relationship. And just as there are few differences between homosexual and heterosexual couples, so there are few—if any—differences between homosexual and heterosexual parents.

Also, there is no evidence that shows that living with a homosexual parent has any significant negative effect on the development of children.

Families as a System

The family can be said to be a social system that has its own unique features and characteristics. Family therapists and other experts who study the family often use a family systems approach when trying to understand the dynamics in a group. These therapists and researchers use the general systems theory that describes families as operating in ways that are similar to the way other systems in nature operate.

ESSENTIAL

The American family is also undergoing economic stress. Nearly twenty million children live in poverty. About 8 percent of all children live in extreme poverty. The majority of indigent families live in substandard housing without adequate health care, nutrition, or child care.

What many people find helpful is the way systems theory is useful in explaining the complex interactions of a family and the factors that influence the processes by which a family makes decisions, sets and achieves particular goals, and establishes rules that regulate behavior. Systems theory also helps to explain how a family responds to change—not only to developmental changes of children or parents—but to various other changes that challenge the functioning of the family as a group.

Essentially, systems theory says that the complex relationships within a family can be understood, and that when change takes place, the reactions of various family members will follow certain rules or patterns. However, the ultimate goal of a family system, so say family system theorists, is to maintain stability or equilibrium over time. Family systems therapists would try to help bring about stability by suggesting changes that will impact all other members and the therapists hope that this impact will be positive and will reestablish harmony.

The Family and Parenting Skills

Children raised by parents who lack proper parenting skills are more at risk than those whose parents are supportive and who provide effective control. While some parents are effective authority figures, others are overly permissive and indulgent, while still others are repressive and strict. Permissive, disengaged parents and punitive parents have been associated with children who displayed negative behaviors.

ALERT

Parents of children with serious behavior problems have been found to be inconsistent in their ability to set rules. They are also less likely to show interest in their kids, and they often display high levels of hostile detachment.

Parents who rely solely on authoritarian discipline practices may be less successful than parents who are firm, consistent, and nurturing with their children. When parents maintain a "my way or the highway" approach to parenting, or when they tell their kids that "as long as you live under my roof you will obey my rules," there is a greater likelihood for parent-child conflict and for inadequate communication. Along with conflict and poor communication, children who live with parents with these views will often be rebellious.

Parenting Styles

There is no magic formula to parenting. In general, parents have to adapt their methods to each child's temperament and needs as well as to the demands of the family and the culture.

However, each child in a family will develop differently within that family system. Attachment forms the foundation for later family relationships. But which parenting style is best?

Research shows that warm, responsive parents are generally better at exercising control than are hostile, rejecting parents. Parents who use power-assertive discipline methods that rely heavily on the superior power of the parent or who are demeaning toward the child—by using physical punishment, threats, or humiliation—may have children who come to see themselves as helpless or unworthy. In some instances, children of power-assertive parents may turn on their parent or on others with aggression.

What Parents Bring to Parenting

Most parents come to the job of parenting with some ideas about the qualities or traits they would like to see their child develop, along with ideas about the childrearing qualities that would encourage the attributes they desire.

There are various pathways for raising children successfully—as well as unsuccessfully. But two important things parents bring to the rearing of their children are emotionality and control.

Emotionality

Parents bring emotions to their role as parents. In general, parents can be either warm and loving or cold and rejecting. Warm and nurturing parents are likely to be responsive to their child's needs. Research shows that children with loving and warm parents feel good about themselves, may be less anxious, and are more likely to feel secure. In addition, children with warm and nurturing parents are more likely to learn and to accept and internalize parental standards than are children of rejecting parents. On the other hand, parents who are cold and rejecting may cause anxiety in their child and those children may have greater difficulty learning the social rules.

Control

Parents have control over their young children, and at the same time they are trying to teach their children to have self-control. Some research indicates that parents must be in control in order that the family is functional. A dysfunctional, chaotic family will have negative effects on a child. But how a parent exercises control is important. If a parent uses suggestions and reasoning and at the same time presents possible alternative courses of action, the child is more likely to be cooperative with the parent's wishes.

If a parent is consistent in her discipline, uses minimal amounts of pressure to bring about a change in a child's behavior, and encourages the child to view his compliance as self-initiated, then children are more likely to cooperate and to internalize the parent's standards.

The Role of Siblings

More than 80 percent of American families have more than one child. The number of children in a family can influence the family system in various ways: the gender of the children, the spacing of the children, and the relationships among the children. As it turns out, in families with more than one child, siblings tend to spend more time interacting with each other than they do with their parents. The siblings, therefore, form their own system within the larger system of the family. Sibling relationships are key to many feelings and problems within the family. However, the bonds that form between brothers and sisters often remain strong for the rest of each individual's life.

Birth Order

A child's position in the family affects her, her siblings, her parents, and the interactions of all family members. Experts think that the position of each child has a major influence on personality and on socialization throughout childhood.

Firstborn children seem to have many advantages. They have the exclusive attention of their parents until the second child comes along. And because of this great amount of attention the firstborn receives, they often are adult-oriented, helpful, self-controlled, studious, conscientious, and serious. They often excel in academics and professional achievements.

Second-born children may be more innovative and more willing to challenge the status quo than their older siblings. They also tend to be less anxious than firstborn children.

Only children tend to be adult-oriented. They are often high achievers, they are frequently more mature than other children, and they often demonstrate leadership skills.

Besides having an influence on the way each child develops, birth order also changes the role of parents. While parents devote considerable attention to their firstborn child, they do not give as much attention to the oldest child after siblings are born. Also, as it turns out, fathers get more involved in parenting when second and third children are born. And a mother often becomes more coercive toward an older child when she is caring for a younger sibling. Also, a mother is less playful with the oldest child than she was before siblings were born.

What about Sibling Rivalry?

Sibling rivalry is a fact of life. Just ask any parent who has two or more children. Sibling rivalry and jealousy can start very young. Usually there are rather obvious signs that a child is feeling jealous of a newly arrived sibling. When toddlers or preschoolers act in an aggressive manner toward a younger sibling, it is usually because they resent sharing the spotlight with a new brother or sister, or because they resent being ignored or left out. And when young children regress in their behavior (by, for instance, insisting that they be fed out of a bottle, crying more frequently, or by suddenly having more toileting accidents), the regression can be related to the arrival of a new sibling.

But sibling rivalry doesn't happen because parents didn't do a good job of preparing their firstborn for a new baby. Most parents do a great job of trying to help young children be aware of and accepting a new baby in the family. Parents these days are very much aware of the need to make sure older children know a baby is coming and to understand that they will be sharing their life with a new child.

However, no matter how well parents prepare children for a new baby, an older child may never really be fully prepared for the changes that are likely to take place in the family when a new baby comes along. For parents, it may be exhausting caring for a new baby around the clock, and this sometimes means that an older child doesn't get nearly the attention she once did.

ESSENTIAL

What can parents do when they recognize that a child feels jealousy or anger? It is important, initially, to be aware that despite your best efforts, sibling rivalry will very likely happen. It might not be apparent in the first few days, but in the later weeks and months it may show up—and once it does it could go on for months.

Parents need to give their older child as much time and attention as possible. While parents of a newborn baby may be sleep deprived and be very concerned about the baby's settling into sleep and eating routines, the older child needs to be reminded that he is still loved.

Many children regress as they feel left out, so they go backward in their development and in their needs. Parents should be tolerant of this for a while, and if the older child needs to be cuddled more and treated like a younger child, he should be indulged.

Parent Pointers for Handling Sibling Rivalry

When parents recognize that an older child is jealous of a new baby in the family, they can look for opportunities to point out that the baby loves the older child too. An older child may not always feel so loving toward the new kid in the family, but he will feel better if he begins to believe the baby likes him.

Because envious and jealous older siblings may be not only angry but also aggressive with an infant, parents can teach affectionate alternatives to aggression. Many young children act in angry and aggressive ways toward the baby they see as an intruder in their lives. While parents need to protect the baby, they also need to teach the older child how to show gentleness and kindness when his aggression gets the better of him.

Another tip is to try to enlist the older child's help. Let him hold the baby, feed the infant a bottle, or help out when the baby is given a bath. Finally, parents can help the older child label his unpleasant feelings. They can let him know that jealousy is normal and all older children feel jealousy at some times. But they can let him know that no matter how he feels about the baby, his parents will continue to love him anyway.

Divorce and Child Development

Estimates show that nearly one million divorces take place each year in this country. Further, somewhere between 20 and 30 percent of these divorces continue into high-conflict relationships. That means that hundreds of thousands of children each year join the ranks of those children from previous divorces (and separations) who have to endure the ongoing fighting and arguing of their parents.

While it is not certain about the exact number of high-conflict, post-divorce relationships, it is more certain what happens to children exposed to prolonged and intense conflict between their parents. Children whose parents continue to fight after the first or second year following a divorce will experience a number of devastating consequences, including physical changes (such as increased blood pressure and increased stress levels), anxiety and depression, acting-out behaviors, and academic problems at school.

Parents in a high-conflict relationship with a former spouse or partner can pay attention to some important "don'ts" in order to protect and shield their child from the effects of high conflict:

- Don't put the child in the middle of the bickering and squabbling of coparents.
- Don't use a child as a go-between. Messages to be conveyed between coparents should be transmitted directly—not through a child.

- Don't discuss adult issues with a child. Areas that you should never discuss with a child include custody, child support, and parenting time.
- Don't make a child a parent's confidant. Children should not be placed in the position of having to take care of their parents—emotionally or otherwise. Nor should children be expected to help solve their parents' problems.
- Don't bad-mouth the other coparent in front of a child. No matter how tempting it is to let a child know what their other parent is really like, parents should avoid this temptation.
- Don't place a child in a situation where she is likely going to have to lie to one of her parents in order to show her love. That may mean not asking questions about what is going on at the other house or asking about the personal life of the other parent.

Many divorced parents have done one or more of these; however, when parents recognize that what they are doing is harmful, they should stop so that they may not cause any more damage their child.

Maintaining Contact with the Noncustodial Parent

Parents who limit contacts by their coparent with the children often have what they believe to be rational reasons. Yet, children suffer when they are deprived of the very important regular contact that they should have with their noncustodial parent.

Research has found that many children of divorce have infrequent contact with their noncustodial parent. Some studies have pointed out that about a third of noncustodial fathers see their children only once a week. And a similar percentage of noncustodial fathers only communicate with their children by phone or letter once a week. Other surveys have shown that about one in five fathers has not seen his children in the past year.

But there is convincing research that demonstrates that children need regular contact with their noncustodial parents. Children view their noncustodial parents as important in their lives and children have been found to be better adjusted when they have regular contacts with both parents following a divorce. In fact, one study discovered that the more frequent the contact between the noncustodial parent and the child, the stronger the relationship between that parent and the kids.

ALERT

The lack of frequent contacts between a child and his noncustodial parent often has a lot to do with money. However, this is an issue that cuts both ways. Coparents who don't get to see their children very often may get revenge by not paying child support regularly. On the other hand, noncustodial parents who do have frequent contacts with their children are more likely to make regular child support payments.

Contacts Between Children and Parents

No matter how a divorced parent feels about his coparent, it is important for the overall well-being of children that there be frequent contacts with both parents. When one parent interferes with the parenting-time relationship between a child and another parent, it may hurt that other coparent, but it is hurting the child even more. When coparents have issues with each other, they must find alternatives to dealing with the issues other than by making the child a pawn in the conflict. Adult issues should not be played out through children. Responsible parents try to protect their children; they do not expose them to the emotional turmoil and hurt of the discord between two parents.

Single Parenting

Many people still think of the traditional and most healthy family as a father, a mother, and one or more children living together in a home. However, that kind of "ideal" family is slowly disappearing in America. Actually, less than 20 percent of families represent this ideal family form.

With the increasing rate of divorce, there are ever-increasing single-parent families; however, single-parent families also result from separations, death of one parent, having children without marriage, and parents who prefer to parent alone.

Frequently, it seems that the problems and challenges faced by single parents overshadow the strengths of a single-parent family. Some of the challenges include economic stresses, problems with child care, and difficulties trying to carry out the myriad tasks that come with raising children.

Yet, there are strengths in single families, too. For example, women often say that single-parenting helped to build personal strengths and confidence. And some single parents say that it is easier to establish communication within a single-parent household. Fathers frequently say that being a single father forced them to become more attentive and loving dads.

Maternal Employment

Since the 1970s, increasing numbers of mothers have been entering the workforce. Has this had an effect on children, though? One area that has undoubtedly had an impact on children is that of the role model for children. When mothers play a greater role in the economic life of the family, there will be changes in other aspects of the family system. For example, with mothers working more and contributing to the family's finances, father participation in child care and household chores has increased. However, even with a significant increase in fathers' participation, it is still true that mothers still must play a major role in both areas—child care and household chores. The effect on children is that they are less likely to see mothers and fathers in the strict traditional roles. That then means that children grow up learning that there is an inequality in the roles both parents play in the home.

FACT

Research shows that there is no long-term negative effect on children's development when mothers are employed outside the home. The most likely impact on children will come from the individual differences of mothers—not from the fact that they are either working or not working.

It is not whether a mother or a father works a fulltime job or has a career. Rather, it is the nature of a parent's job that matters for kids. For instance, a parent's experience of stress on the job may play a role in the life of a child, or even in the individual parent's personal life or the marriage. Both mothers and fathers who are in high-stress jobs may withdraw from their children when they are home and they may be more irritable and less able to have a warm and caring relationship with their child.

CHAPTER 11

Peers, Play, and Learning

For both adults and children, play is fun. However, for kids, play has its serious side as well. For children, play is a means of connecting with the world. And although different children play in different ways, play serves the same purpose for all children. Although the nature of play changes as children grow, play still remains central to the healthy emotional and physical growth of children. Some child development experts refer to play as children's main way of communicating, expressing, and learning. It would not be an exaggeration to say that play is the foundation for everything that comes later in a child's life.

What Is Play?

Play has been defined as children's work. Some people say that play is everything young children do when they are not sleeping or being directed by adults. Likewise, play is whenever kids are following their own imagination and directing their own activities.

Play consists of a great deal more than stacking blocks or playing baseball. It is more than a toddler pushing a toy car or truck; it's more than a young teen playing a video game. In effect, play is doing whatever younger children choose to do and it's what older children and teens do with their friends.

Parenting expert William Sears has written that play is doing rather than watching. For Sears, play involves the senses—hearing, feeling, and seeing. At its best, play offers choices and it provides different ways for children to explore their environment and explore problems.

FACT

Through play children get to test their skills and abilities. Since they can do this in relatively safe and benign ways, they typically don't feel overwhelmed. When they can engage in play with their peers and away from adults, children can work on being independent and autonomous while gaining a feeling of power over situations. Play is how children gain a sense of mastery.

What Are the Different Kinds of Play?

Play includes a wide range of activities. Play can vary from children stacking wooden blocks or pretending to drive cars to playing tea party with dolls. It can involve building airplanes with Legos or throwing a ball or pushing a mobile to see how it moves. In older children it can revolve around a pick-up game of kickball or basketball, or it can feature the competition of a video game among friends. A game of Monopoly is play for older children, and for teens it may mean eating with buddies at a fast-food restaurant or just hanging out.

Play changes depending on a child's age. Teachers and child-care staff describe parallel play when children play in the same room but do not really play together. As kids get older, for example preschool age, they tend to play together. And as they get in the school-age years their play becomes more organized and often involves strict rules.

Whether kids realize it or not, they are playing most of the time. But the importance of all this play is that it helps children develop competence and mastery of the world around them; play helps children foster close emotional relationships, and play helps them recover after emotional distress.

Play Fosters Close Emotional Relationships

Although it may not always seem like it to adults, a part of children's play is about building emotional closeness to their peers. By playing together, children express their emotions and they learn how to deal with their emotions in a safe and fun setting.

On a day-to-day basis, children experience many kinds of hurts, slights, and emotional trauma. Perhaps their traumas are not so serious from an adult perspective, but still for children they are emotional hurts. But children and adults recover in different ways from emotional trauma. Adults may talk to others about how they were hurt; children can use play. Play permits youngsters to recover because they can engage in a favorite activity and at the same time they can use the safety of a play situation to "play out" the emotional trauma or hurt. While adults may talk it out, children play it out.

Play Dates and Play Groups

Initially, a baby's play partners are her parents. It is parents who smile, make funny faces, produce strange noises by blowing on an infant's stomach, or teach her how to roll a ball or play patty cake.

However, as babies grow into the toddler stage and they learn how to walk, perhaps run, and talk, their parents often want them to learn to play with other children. That frequently leads parents to arrange or schedule play dates with other parents and their similar-aged children. Of course, parents are disappointed—sometimes even shocked or embarrassed—to realize their toddler is not very good at playing with peers. During the toddler stage, young children often seem to have no interest in interacting with their peers, may refuse to share their toys, or they may attack new friends with aggressive hitting, pushing, or biting.

But with parent help and support, and over time, young children learn how to share and how to relate to other children without hitting them or biting them. They become more adept at playing in a cooperative fashion with each other. As they move forward into the school-age years they begin to be friendlier in play situations. It is during the elementary school years that play helps children develop close friendships and form bonds with each other.

How Dads Play

As anyone who has ever watched mothers and fathers play with their infants and toddlers will realize, there is a distinct difference in the play of each sex. Dads are far more physical, swinging, bouncing, throwing, and stimulating their children.

According to Ross Parke, a pioneering psychologist who has helped emphasize the importance of fathers, the area in which fathers' parenting styles are most obviously different from mothers' is in play. Parke's research has revealed that fathers engage in a special and uniquely stimulating approach to play with their children. Dads play in a much more physical way than do mothers. Fathers' play styles tend to stress competition, challenge, initiative, risk-taking, and independence.

QUESTION

Isn't the way my husband plays with our daughter likely to overstimulate her and make her more aggressive?
Children actually love the physical kind of play they engage in with their fathers. It is a stimulating kind of play, but there is no research to show that it overstimulates children or causes any emotional or psychological damage at all.

Psychologists have pointed out that Dad's physical style of play affects everything from the child's management of impulses to intelligence and academic achievement. Studies show that physical play helps children develop the social skills they need to get along well with their peers. Children who roughhouse with their dads learn how to control their impulses and their aggression. During play with their children, especially when that play gets rough or children get too aggressive or angry, dads can model self-regulation and can modify the way they respond by reacting in controlled ways. Fathers, therefore, teach their children, both boys and girls, to handle their aggression in appropriate ways.

Child Care and Play

Today about two million or more children are in some form of child care provided by someone other than their parents. The types of child care available to parents vary extensively from day care provided by a large center with elaborate facilities to informal care in a private home—and everything in between. These forms of child care can be called day care, nursery school, preschool, or even just plain baby-sitting.

But whatever child care is called, it is very evident that the quality of the care also varies. High-quality child care tends to encourage children to be actively engaged in a variety of activities, to have frequent and positive interactions with caregivers as well as other children, and to encourage children to express their experiences, feelings, and ideas—both verbally and ultimately in writing. In addition, quality child care involves providing children with a safe environment, access to age-appropriate toys, and participation in free play and age-appropriate play activities.

The Learning Process

Children are active learners. This is evident from the moment of birth—and maybe, even earlier, during the fetal stage of pregnancy. Initially, they may learn for the most part through their visual and auditory senses, but as they acquire mobility and language children have a great ability to influence their own learning. They do this by exploring their environment and interacting with parents, siblings, and peers.

Although attending preschool is gradually becoming the norm for children in the United States, there can be many variations in the way children are introduced to education and more formal learning. It seems clear to developmental psychologists that children learn best through active, hands-on teaching methods. Whether they are learning at home, in a day care, preschool, or nursery school, children need a safe but stimulating environment with exposure to books and reading, with the encouragement to explore their environment, and to have access to consistent and responsive adults.

To best stimulate learning, children should be challenged at a level just beyond their current mastery and they need new opportunities to practice newly acquired skills. Some day cares and preschools may provide opportunities for more challenging play while others may not understand that challenge is important if children are going to make advances.

Day Cares and Preschools

Many children attend day care centers and preschools, and many, if not most, parents choose a day care or a preschool based on an expectation that the experience will provide a favorable academic foundation that will lead to advantages in elementary school and beyond.

Some experts say that children will learn best if the school focuses on facilitating children's social and emotional development while also helping children to develop their cognitive skills. Schools that provide such a focus are referred to by educators as ones that provide a developmentally appropriate education. The emphasis in a developmentally appropriate educational program will be on helping young children think critically, work cooperatively, solve problems, develop self-regulation skills, and enjoy learning.

ESSENTIAL

The National Association for the Education of Young Children (NAEYC) has a publication entitled "Developmentally Appropriate Practice," which describes the requirements for a high-quality, developmentally focused program. That publication and others can be purchased from the NAEYC website at *www.naeyc.org.*

Many, but certainly not all, students show significant positive benefits from a developmentally appropriate education. The problems with doing definitive research on this question of how many children benefit and to what extent is that preschools and programs for young children vary considerably in curriculum and quality, and to make matters worse, the whole idea of what constitutes a developmentally appropriate education is still evolving.

How can a parent tell if a preschool has a developmentally appropriate curriculum? According to the Yale University Child Study Center, the success of a preschool depends on the ability of its director and staff to develop a close relationship with and maintain excellent communication with parents. It's important to choose a preschool program where parents feel comfortable asking for help, sharing observations of their children, and working closely with teachers. Furthermore, parents should determine that the director and staff have educational backgrounds in child development and early childhood education. The program should have goals and a philosophy that are implemented by a curriculum that is developmentally appropriate. In general, the curriculum in a preschool program should reflect that teachers have an understanding of what children of each age and stage need to learn in terms of various skills, information, and concepts.

The Importance of Teachers in Child Development

There is no question that the teacher is the most important component in the school as far as young children are concerned. Of course, teachers set the pace in the classroom, they develop the curriculum for the class, and they determine how learning materials will be presented.

In both the preschool and the elementary classroom, the teacher is a substitute parent. For instance, the excellent teacher will provide students emotional support, will transmit values, will encourage appropriate behaviors, and will discourage inappropriate behaviors. Beyond that, it is very important that students like their teacher. And it is clear that young students do like certain teachers over others. Research shows that the teachers students like best are kind, considerate, sympathetic, interested in students as people, fair, flexible, interested, and committed. As it turns out, popular and well-liked teachers are often able to bring out the best in their students. In addition, children often emulate the behavior of teachers they like.

Many successful people attribute their achievements to a favorite teacher. It is true that parents often serve as role models for their children, but it is equally true that a teacher may provide the spark or inspiration that makes the difference in an individual's life. When teachers recognize the potential in a child or they help a young person see talents and abilities no one else has brought to the child's attention, a young person may begin to believe in his own possibilities. A beloved teacher can make a world of difference in the life of a child.

The Importance of Peers

Between the ages of six and twelve, children spend an average of just over 40 percent of their waking hours in the company of peers. This amount of time is about double what it was in the preschool years. Obviously, with an increase in the time spent playing with peers, there is a corresponding decrease in the amount of time spent with parents.

But time spent with peers is different from time spent with parents. When children are with their parents, their parents tend to preside over the activities of children. When parents direct children's activities, some form of instruction is often involved. However, when kids are playing together, they are likely to play a game or just hang out together with no instruction. Also, when children are with parents, parents tend to keep a watchful eye and make sure there is order and control. However, when with their peers, there is no person in control and there is no central authority figure. The authority has to be established by children themselves, and, in general, any such authority is established through negotiation, compromise, and discussion.

Peers, Games, and Rules

In the middle-childhood years, children may play fantasy games in which roles are assigned. These can be games like being a family, cops and robbers, or school. But in the school-age years a new form of play comes along—games based on rules.

After about ages seven or eight, fantasy games tend to fade in the background and rules become the essence of many, if not most, games. One aspect of rule-based games is that children must use cognitive skills to remember the rules, which are sometimes very detailed and elaborate. Furthermore, children now need to engage in social perspective-taking, which means they have to understand the relation between the thoughts of the other players and their own actions.

Also, the goals of rule-based games change. In earlier fantasy play, the goal was in the fantasy and the roles children played. In rule-based games, the objective is often to win through competition based on the rules.

The Importance of Rules

In the middle-childhood years, children try to win according to the rules of the game. Early in this period of development, children regard rules with awe and tend to believe that some greater authority established the rules and those rules must never be changed. By ages nine or ten, kids may be less in awe of the rules and they begin to realize that rules are established by mutual consent. While they still believe that rules are very important, they can see that, if all the players decide to change the rules, that change is permissible. But once the rules are changed, everyone must agree to abide by the rules.

Thinking about rules leads children to consider the role of rules not only in games but in life. It is near the end of the middle-childhood years that children consider the morality of rules. Breaking a rule is like being immoral. And there is the aspect of fairness. At ages ten and eleven, fairness is extremely important. Anyone who breaks a rule is being unfair, and it doesn't matter whether that person is an adult or a peer. For children it is just not right when someone fails to follow established rules.

Peers and Friendships

Parents and siblings are important agents of socialization throughout childhood. But, peers are also important in transmitting socialization during the preschool years. For instance, social play during the early years actually helps children. There is research that suggests that social play gives children not just enjoyment and physical exercise. In addition, some studies say, children who are deprived of social play with preschool peers have more difficulty understanding other children's points of view and have more difficulty getting along with friends and peers.

There is no doubt that peers play an important role in adolescent development; however, the function of adolescent peer groups is virtually the same for teens as it was for younger children. Children at all ages use their peer group for social interaction; they use the peer group to develop skills appropriate for their age, and they use the peer group to share similar problems and feelings.

During the teenage years, though, peer group relations generally take on one of three forms:

- The crowd
- The clique
- The individual friendship

Cliques, Crowds, and Individual Friendships

There are many children who do not feel comfortable in cliques or crowds but still have friends. These friendships may be based on individual friendships. That is, two peers may be friends, but only one or neither belongs to a clique or a crowd. This may well be the predominant kind of peer relationship in elementary school or even in middle school. However, this type of relationship may be less often the case in high school where belonging to a crowd or a clique may be important for teens who are trying to figure who they are and where they belong.

Three types of cliques have been identified by experts in most high schools across the United States. They are the intellectuals (kids who are academically oriented), the delinquents (teens who are hoods, the tough kids, and those who avoid classes), and the socialites (the well-known adolescents who are popular, and tend to admire the jocks or the athletes).

The crowd is the largest and least personal group of adolescents. It generally comprises teens who are interested in the same activities but not necessarily in each other. For example, a crowd may be a group of adolescents who enjoy going to sports events at their school, but who do not all go together, nor do they necessarily sit in the same section or get together afterward. Yet, one of the favorite activities of a crowd is "hanging out."

A clique, on the other hand, is a smaller and more intimate group of people than a crowd. Cliques tell each other about crowd activities, share information about current styles, and tend to show similar interests in current topics of conversation. Cliques typically reinforce their member's values and they promote their own norms or behavioral standards. For example, a clique may be the skateboarders at a certain high school.

The Diminishing Influence of the Peer Group

By their senior year, the influence of the peer group clique has generally diminished for many, if not most, high school students. As teens get older, they are more self-assured and secure about their place in high school society. By the time they are in the final year of high school, youth tend to rely on their own decision-making skills rather than looking to a clique to help them decide what to do.

ALERT

When children are neglected or overlooked by their peers, they frequently feel lonely and hostile. Experiencing rejection and neglect from peers over several years in childhood is related to an individual's subsequent mental health and whether or not the child becomes involved in criminal activity.

How Peers Help—and Hurt—Kids

Good peer relations may be necessary for normal social development. That is, it may be difficult for any child to grow up healthy and well-adjusted if he has no friends or has no social relationships. When children are socially isolated and are not able to find their way into any social relationships or any social network, then those children are likely to be susceptible to certain kinds of problems and disorders; these may range from depression to problem drinking to delinquency.

In general, peer relations can be both positive and negative. Studies show that having adequate peer relationships in the school years is linked to work success and satisfying romantic relationships in early adulthood. Furthermore, popularity with peers and a low level of aggression at age eight foreshadows high occupational status in later adulthood.

The quality of peer relationships for teenagers is particularly important. Poor peer relations are strongly linked to depression, drug use, and delinquency in adolescents. Studies have shown that time spent hanging out with antisocial peers during the teen years is a stronger predictor of substance abuse than is time spent with parents. Also, adolescents who hang around with deviant peers are more likely to be depressed.

CHAPTER 12

Personality

In the first few months of life, an infant does not come across as a unique person. In other words, there is no sense of self. A baby can be aware of sensations, such as warmth, pain, and hunger, but she is not yet able to distinguish between what happens inside her body versus what happens outside her body. Perhaps the first real step toward development of a self—or a personality—comes about when an infant forms a close bond with her caregiver. This bonding, or attachment, leads to a secure child who eventually has her own way of responding to people and events in her world. It's this unique way of responding that gives her a personality.

What Is Personality?

Personality is an individual's unique way of reacting to others and to events. Personality might also be defined as the multitude of emotions, behaviors, and attitudes that characterize each person and makes that person different from every other person.

And how does each person's personality develop? In the first half of the twentieth century, the prevailing view by psychologists was that personality was permanently molded by the actions of the parents, most especially the mother, during the early years of childhood. There were two major theoretical versions of how personality was molded:

- **The learning theory point of view:** The learning theorists said that personality was molded based on parents' reinforcing or punishing their child's behavior.
- **The psychoanalytic theory point of view:** The psychoanalysts said that an individual's personality was formed in the first few years of life and that the mother played a pivotal role in terms of how children resolved each of the important stages of psychosexual development.

While both theories have been influential, today most psychologists believe that it is the overall pattern of parental warmth and sensitivity that strongly affects a child's emotional development and leads to personality traits. However, most psychologists also believe that heredity also plays a prominent role in the development of personality.

The Factors That Shape Personality

There are two primary factors that come together to shape an individual's personality. Those two factors are heredity and the environment. Although many psychologists in the past assumed that both heredity and the environment play a role in personality, more recently studies suggest that the prenatal environment as well as environmental factors at birth may make a greater contribution to infant temperament than do heredity and genetics. Temperament is the basic style with which a person responds to the environment, and it includes the dominant mood of each person.

Personality traits show some stability over time, which might suggest a genetic influence, yet many psychologists agree that both heredity and environmental factors contribute to personality.

FACT

Psychological research reveals that identical twins are more alike than are fraternal twins in their responses to strangers and in such behaviors as smiling, playing, cuddling, and the expression of fear. Identical twins also appear more alike than fraternal twins in the frequency of displays of temper, demands for attention, and the amount of crying they do.

Research shows that heredity contributes to individual differences in a number of temperamental characteristics and personality traits. For example, studies indicate that heredity likely plays a large role in people's having varying degrees of the following traits: emotionality, fear and anxiety, activity level, attention span, persistence, a tendency to maintain high moral standards, and a tendency to obey authority.

Social Influences on Personality

It is difficult to separate social and emotional development from personality formation. Social development may be defined as the developmental process in which children simultaneously become integrated into the larger social community and differentiated as distinctive people. But there are two aspects of social development. One is socialization, in which children acquire the standards, values, and knowledge of their society. The second is personality formation, in which children come to have a characteristic sense of themselves and distinctive ways of thinking and feeling.

Socialization during early childhood is especially important because this is when kids construct their first understanding of the community. Adults play a critical role in this process as they tell children how they are expected to behave and also reward and punish their behavior. But socialization also involves a child's understanding of the social categories, roles, rules, and expectations that allow him to interact in appropriate ways with others. Thus, the roles and the behaviors a child learns from this process can be said to be a part of personality.

However, it is a combination of characteristics that emerge from the second aspect of social development, personality formation, that helps to make each child unique. It is a mixture of genetic endowment and personal experiences that helps to bring about personality traits, even though some elements of personality are apparent shortly after birth. These are often the temperamental traits. But personality is much more than the temperamental traits that make up the unique way infants respond to the world. Personality development is very closely intertwined with socialization and the myriad of biological and social events each child experiences.

ALERT

There is a set of positive personality traits associated with secure attachment between parent and child. In contrast, children with insecure or anxious attachments tend to be preoccupied with their teachers. They spend more time than their peers seeking guidance, support, and discipline from their teachers. They also spend more time sitting on their teachers' laps during group activities.

Day Care and Its Impact on Personality

Day care has an influence on the developing child, but the most clear-cut influence has to do with the developing personality of young children. Children who attend day care centers tend to be:

- More self-sufficient
- More independent of parents and teachers
- More helpful and cooperative with peers and parents
- More verbally expressive
- More knowledgeable about the social world
- More comfortable in new situations

While there are many positive outcomes for children when they attend a day care program during early childhood, there are also some negative effects. In some instances, children who have attended day care centers have been rated as less polite, less agreeable, less compliant with adults, and more aggressive than children who have not been in day care. These effects, some experts contend, may vary based on the quality of day care and the involvement of the child's parents.

Early and Late Maturation and Its Effect on Personality

In general, early maturing boys, that is, boys who experience puberty early, seem to have a more favorable attitude toward their own bodies and they are often seen by others as more mature psychologically and socially. Other research shows that early sexual maturation is associated with lower self-control and less emotional stability. Boys who reach puberty at a relatively early age are those boys who are more likely to smoke, drink, use drugs, and get in trouble with the law during adolescence.

The outlook for early maturing girls is even less positive than for early maturing boys. In some cases, early maturation brings greater social pressure for girls because of their sexual attractiveness. When girls go through puberty early, they may experience social difficulties because their physical development leads boys to pressure them into sexual relationships that they are not ready for psychologically. Some research indicates that early maturing girls experience somewhat lower emotional stability and lower levels of self-control than late maturing girls. They are also more likely to get into trouble with adults because of increased truancy, smoking, drinking, and defiant behavior, and to have fewer years of schooling. However, while late-maturing girls may have negative feelings about themselves, as they reach later adolescence they may experience more satisfaction with their appearance and be more popular with their early maturing peers.

Attachment May Preview Personality Traits

An infant's attachment pattern may be a preview of the child's social and personality development in the years to come. For instance, securely attached infants tend to become children who interact with teachers in friendly and appropriate ways. In addition, securely attached babies may turn out to be those children who seek help when it is needed and who are competent in a wide array of social and cognitive skills. Psychologists point out that attachment is not the cause of these later traits, but they are a sign of the direction a child's development may take.

Sociability May Be Inherited

Sociability, or introversion/extroversion, involves the nature of the child's interaction with others. A sociable child is one who is outgoing and enjoys being around people. Research suggests that sociability may have a genetic origin and that it appears early in infancy and remains very stable over the course of childhood. Sociability in boys is particularly stable since both introversion and extroversion seems to change little after the first year of life.

Irritability May Be Another Inherited Trait

Some infants are more irritable than others, while some are quite calm and placid. The irritability or the soothe-ability of a baby may be apparent when a child is just a few days old. The easily irritated baby may be viewed as the fussy infant. These babies don't just cry a lot; they have a variety of extreme responses that make them generally more difficult to deal with. Many factors have been suggested for this extreme fussiness, but so far no one theory has been supported by scientific evidence. This absence of one clear cause may strongly suggest that fussiness is inherited.

Other Personality Traits Influenced by Genetic Factors

Although sociability and irritability may have genetic components, there are other personality traits that also appear to be inherited. These other traits include:

- Activity level
- Rhythmicity
- Adaptability
- Intensity of reactions
- Distractibility

- Attention span and persistence
- Threshold of responsiveness
- Mood

Temperament and Changes as Children Mature

Temperament, or the typical mode of response to the environment by a child, is inborn and is often apparent in some respects immediately after birth. But temperament is expressed in different ways as an individual grows older. For instance, in early childhood a short attention span may be viewed as the easy distractibility of a young child. In the elementary years, a short attention may be seen as a detriment to focusing on a task in school. However, in adolescence, a person with a short attention span might be described as flighty, spontaneous, or ditzy.

Parents of infants and young children who were rated as difficult report a higher rate of developmental problems in their children later in life. This connection may be related to problems in attachment since difficult babies may be harder for mothers to deal with and mothers of difficult babies may experience greater stress. Too, difficult infants and younger children may elicit adverse reactions both from parents and others. Thus, temperament from a very early age is likely to affect personality development.

Gender and Personality

Early in life, boys and girls are different when it comes to behavior and aspects of their personalities. For instance, boys are generally more aggressive and more often the victims of aggression. Girls, on the other hand, tend to use more indirect forms of aggression such as excluding another child from social play or interaction. As early as two years of age, girls are more likely to comply with the demands of their parents and other adults. Boys at that early age are more inconsistent in their response to adult direction.

Masculinity and femininity not only appear to develop early, but they tend to be a stable personality characteristic. In boys, childhood sexuality and aggression are predictive of adult sexuality and anger. In girls, childhood passivity predicts similar adult behaviors.

Parents Influence Gender

Although hormones play a very important role in **gender role**, gender behavior, and gender traits, it appears that parents do play some role—however slight—in the way a child behaves as either a boy or a girl. For instance, as soon as children are born, each is given a name—one that sounds appropriate for a male or a female—and the child is dressed in clothes that may be blue for a boy or pink for a girl. This, then, is the beginning of the parents' role in shaping different behaviors in boys and girls.

The parental role continues beyond the clothes parents buy and the names that were chosen. A child's view of himself is somewhat shaped by the toys children are given to play with, the decoration scheme in his bedroom, the way his hair is styled, and the words parents say. By the time a child is a toddler, it is firmly established in a child's mind whether he sees himself as a boy or she views herself as a girl.

The expectations that are established in the home also have a distinct bearing on the child's **gender identity**. Boys are expected to be independent, assertive, dominant, and competitive in various kinds of relationships. When boys behave in these ways early in life, they are given positive feedback. If they do not behave in these ways, there is often negative feedback. Girls, on the other hand, are expected to be relatively passive, loving, sensitive, and supportive of others in social relationships. People, including not only parents but other adults as well, expect that girls will suppress their anger and aggression, and their sexuality.

Parents play an indirect role in gender shaping as well. For example, fathers who are dominant and decisive in setting limits and dispensing rewards and punishments are likely to have masculine sons. A boy with a weak father and a powerful mother is likely to exhibit feminine characteristics. Both sons and daughters of very masculine fathers are more assertive and less emotionally expressive than are children of men judged as less masculine.

Peers Also Influence Gender

Research with young children reveals that peers display marked reactions when children violate appropriate gender-role behavior. For example, boys who play with dolls at preschool tend to be criticized by their playmates. This criticism or censure tends to be directed more at boys than at girls. Girls in preschool can play with "boy toys" without garnering as much criticism. On the playground in elementary school boys play with boys and girls play with girls. Some research shows that school-age children spend eleven times as much time with their same-gender peers as with opposite-gender peers. This leads to children learning from each other as to what is appropriate behavior for their gender.

Where Does Self-Esteem Come From?

Is self-esteem a personality trait? Is a child's level of self-esteem inborn or does it come about as a result of experiences? Much of the evidence says that self-esteem is rooted in family experiences. Stanley Coopersmith, one of the major researchers in the area of childhood self-esteem, found in his research that school-age children with high self-esteem had parents with high self-esteem, too. Furthermore, he found that children with high self-esteem were treated as responsible individuals by their parents. Mothers in these families were more accepting and positive toward their children. These mothers also were more affectionate and were more likely to praise their children for their accomplishments. It has also been found that parents of children with high self-esteem also set fairly strict and clear limits for their children's behavior.

Girls and Self-Esteem

Girls may have self-esteem issues from an early age as some studies have shown that boys get more positive feedback from their peers, even as early as preschool, than do girls. However, for a girl, high self-esteem seems to be helped by having a close, supportive relationship with her father. Highly successful, competent, self-confident women consistently report that their fathers treated them "like a son." That is, these fathers expected their daughters to do well, taught them skills, and spent lots of time with them.

When fathers are permanently gone because of divorce or death, are unavailable because of military service, or have little or no interest in their children, it is not necessarily girls who suffer the most. Young boys, more so than young girls, may have problems with gender identity and gender role when a father is permanently unavailable.

On the other hand, the effects of parental absence on preadolescent girls may have a delayed effect on girls' gender typing. Father absence may cause adolescent girls to have difficulty relating to other males. In some studies, teenage girls from divorced homes appear to be more sexually precocious and assertive with boys. Girls whose mothers were widowed have been characterized as extremely anxious about their sexuality and as shy and uncomfortable around males.

ALERT

Aside from family warmth and acceptance, two other things parents do also seem to have a significant effect on a child's self-esteem. Children who were repeatedly labeled in negative ways—being called "dumb" or being characterized as "lazy"—often had lower levels of self-esteem. Children who were frequently given positive labels by their parents—being called "smart" or described as being "good at building things"—were those children with higher levels of self-esteem.

Girls learn to be competent and to value and acquire the social skills necessary for effective relationships with boys and men by having ongoing relationships with fathers who are warm, responsive, and masculine. These fathers appreciate and reward their daughter's femininity. Yet, even if such a father is not available or is permanently absent, it helps if the mother characterizes the absent father in positive ways and if the mother displays emotional stability.

Some Gender Differences Are Real; Some Are Not

At birth, girls are physically and neurologically advanced over boys. Girls tend to walk earlier and they typically reach puberty earlier. From infancy through the early school years, girls display superior verbal abilities with clear advantages over boys in terms of vocabulary, reading comprehension, and verbal creativity. But when it comes to aspects of social and emotional development boys are more often the aggressors as well as the victims of aggression. In terms of atypical development, boys are more likely to have genetic defects, physical disabilities, mental retardation, reading disabilities, and speech defects.

But boys and girls are equally social. There are no differences in boys and girls' needs for love and affection. Boys and girls are equally adept at rote learning and accomplishing simple repetitive tasks. They are equal in terms of their needs to achieve in school. There are no real differences in self-esteem, although boys may rate themselves stronger and more powerful while girls view themselves as more competent in social skills.

CHAPTER 13

Defining Normal in an Information Age

With the tremendous advances in the flow of information via cell phone, fax, e-mail, and the Internet, it is easy to see why the current period is labeled an age of information. Children are likely to be overwhelmed with too much information, and technology brings its own set of anxieties. Having access to myriad choices brings its own anxieties and stress.

What Is Normal?

Defining what is normal is a task assigned to each generation. This task requires more than just providing a definition for the word *normal*. Normal can have more than one meaning. For instance, normal can mean healthy or an absence of pathology. This kind of definition goes along with the medical model of evaluating health. In this model, normalcy, or health, is best described as an absence of sickness or an absence of ill health. But then it is necessary to turn to a doctor, perhaps a pediatrician or a psychologist or psychiatrist, to help determine if a particular child is normal.

But there is also another definition of normal that is perhaps equally valid. In this alternate version normal means what most children think or do. For example, if most sixteen-year-olds are consuming an alcoholic drink every thirty days, then that would constitute normal behavior. Using this definition, it doesn't matter whether drinking by sixteen-year-olds is healthy or illegal; it is simply a question of what are most teens doing. The abnormal teen will be the one who is behaving outside the norm.

In child psychology, the study of abnormal behavior is usually referred to as developmental psychopathology. Psychopathology is the study of disorders of the psyche or the mind.

Is It Normal for Children to Be Anxious?

Anxiety and distress are an inevitable part of a baby's or a young child's life. For example, **stranger anxiety** typically begins between seven and ten months of age and continues for a few months. During this time infants show distress when a stranger gets close to them. Occasionally this fear of strangers could include anxiety when a seldom-seen parent or close relative shows up. However, young children get used to strangers by about twelve to fourteen months, although sometimes the stranger anxiety continues longer.

But then, separation anxiety comes along. Distress related to separation from the primary caregiver surfaces between eight and twelve months and peaks at about eighteen or nineteen months. Usually, this anxiety subsides by about age two.

These two anxieties are a part of development, but then so are other anxieties and distresses that may come along as children encounter entering day care, beginning kindergarten, or going from one class to another each year in elementary and middle school.

What Do Parents Worry About?

Parents worry about the childhood disorders they have heard about and the ones they have a smattering of knowledge about. These disorders often are related to attention-deficit/hyperactivity disorder, **autism**, obsessive-compulsive disorder, and oppositional defiant disorder. However, having only cursory information, perhaps obtained from the Internet, does not make a parent qualified to make a diagnosis. Usually parents don't have the medical or psychological background or the experience to see the bigger picture of which other disorders could have some of the same symptoms, or whether the observed symptoms are not symptoms at all, but are normal behaviors. And that ignorance leads to leaping to the wrong conclusions or failing to consider other, and in some cases, much more appropriate diagnoses. The bottom line here is that parents of young children should not try to make a diagnosis on their own. It is likely to cause too much parental anxiety.

Stranger Anxiety

If a twenty-one-month-old child seems to be afraid of strangers, does this mean she has a problem? Is she socially delayed? Or is she likely to have difficulties later in life relating to peers? Parents may know that children become fearful of strangers and timid in new situations. But they often don't know exactly when this stranger anxiety is supposed to appear and when it is typically over.

For example, toddlers between eighteen months and three years are usually exuberant and outgoing. It is only in very new and novel situations that their facial expressions reveal anxiety or concern. They may look sober or worried, may drop their eyes, or they may grab on to their parents or even hide behind either Mom or Dad. At times, if the situation is unlike anything they've encountered before, they may even whimper or cry.

All toddlers react like this at one time or another. For some, though, it may be an attempt to process what is going on; the anxious behavior may last for twenty or thirty minutes before the child starts to feel more relaxed and begin to act like the exuberant tyke he normally is.

Separation Anxiety

All young children can experience separation anxiety at certain times during the infant and toddler ages. For example, at some time after six months of age, a child may show considerable discomfort when the parent or primary caregiver is out of sight. Most young children will become very distressed when a parent goes away. This kind of separation anxiety usually peaks between ten and eighteen months of age, and then seems to fade during the last part of the second year.

But is it normal for children of three, four, or even five, to experience separation anxiety? When a child first goes to a day care center, preschool, or even kindergarten, there may be intense feelings of distress when the parent drops him off for several hours of day care or school. Plenty of children find it very stressful to be left at school by their parent.

But there can be other reasons or situations that seem to rekindle those strong emotions associated with separation anxiety. This may come about at a time long after age one or two and long after a child has seemingly adjusted to separation from a parent.

This new separation anxiety or distress is a phase, but parents need to be aware that a phase can last more than a few days or even more than a few weeks. The phase could last for as long as three or four months.

Normal Anxiety During the School-Age Years

The characteristics of children, such as gender, attitude, and temperament, may play an important role in the emergence of anxiety-based disabilities during the school-age years. For instance, being a girl places a child at risk for anxiety. And a child who has an **insecure attachment** during infancy is more likely in the elementary school years to experience anxiety disorders.

Temperament is also one of the child variables associated with anxieties. The temperamental trait most associated with anxiety is inhibition.

Inhibition involves a unique mix of wariness, arousal, and emotional and behavioral preferences for a given child.

Investigations by psychologist Jerome Kagan and his colleagues describe children at risk for later anxiety as highly inhibited and highly reactive. Particular types of events, such as threat or loss, are often associated with the development of anxiety or depression.

Trauma that threatens the way the family functions, such as domestic violence or being physically or sexually abused, is especially harmful to children. But so, too, are chronic stresses, such as discrimination, schoolwork, family problems, and peer and relationship problems. All of these stresses can, and often do, lead to anxiety.

Normal Anxiety During Adolescence

One thing that makes teens worried is uncertainty. Given the unsettled nature of adolescence, this may be especially problematic for a great many teenagers. Many young and middle teenagers may view themselves as being adrift in a sea of uncertainty, not knowing who they are, where they fit in, who their friends are, how to deal with schoolwork, or how to relate to their parents.

ESSENTIAL

A 2007 survey of the nation's parents found that parents worry about the role of the media: television, inappropriate websites, YouTube, and social-networking sites. They worry about the amount of sex and violence in the media. Two-thirds of parents surveyed in a Kaiser Family Foundation research project said they are very concerned about their children's exposure to inappropriate media content.

Additional risks for teens, often leading to anxiety, are certain kinds of personality patterns resulting in unsatisfactory peer relationships. Teenagers who are ignored or rejected by their peers experience more social anxiety, and it may take many years, very frequently into adulthood, to get over this kind of anxiety.

Should Parents Worry?

The question of whether parents should worry is a fascinating question for three reasons:

1. No amount of worry is going to change their child, make their child more advanced, or solve any problems a parent might think their child has. Parental anxiety, in and of itself, does nothing to help a child.
2. Often what parents tend to worry about could be solved by either more accurate information or by obtaining a professional opinion by an expert in the field related to their concern.
3. Parents could ease their own worries by taking action. For example, while the Kaiser Family Foundation study cited above said two-thirds of parents were very concerned about what children were exposed to in the media, very few parents used the V-Chip that comes in all newer TVs and very few understood the rating systems for TV shows. By taking action, actually using the V-Chip to block objectionable programming, or learning the rating system, parents could ease their worries.

ADHD

Many child psychologists began to recognize in the 1970s and 1980s that a little knowledge could be a dangerous thing—for parents and teachers. That's when there was a growing understanding in our society that many children were hyperactive. Professionals working with children were just beginning to label a disorder that would later be called **attention-deficit/hyperactivity disorder (ADHD)**.

Increasing publicity about ADHD led teachers to tell parents that the reason their child was experiencing school or behavior problems was because the child had ADHD. And parents themselves would take their child to a pediatrician or a mental health professional convinced their child had ADHD. Of course, many such children had neither ADHD nor any other kind of disorder. Some were normal children; others had anxiety related to other issues in their lives.

There are many reasons why a child might appear to be hyperactive or to have ADHD. Some of the myriad of causes of hyperactivity include:

- Normal childhood exuberance
- Anxiety
- Child abuse
- Depression
- Tourette's syndrome
- Behavior problems
- Learning disabilities

QUESTION

My four-year-old son plays with the same toys every day and always lines them up in the same way. Does this mean he has obsessive-compulsive disorder (OCD)?
A great many parents may be worried about this kind of play. Such behavior could be an early sign of OCD, but it could just as easily be normal behavior of a curious child trying to understand objects and their relationships with each other. Children engage in a lot of repetitive play in order to learn about ordering and classification of objects. Children use play to better understand color, size, and other relationships.

If it is true for ADHD that some of the symptoms that are seen in ADHD could also have other causes, then it is also true for many other childhood disorders or problems. For example, other childhood behaviors or disorders that could have various possible causes include:

1. Behavior problems
2. Autism-like symptoms
3. Communication problems
4. Learning problems

To say a child has a learning problem or a behavior problem is not to know or understand anything substantial about that child. Parents, teachers, and professionals in the mental health field should always look beneath the symptoms to determine why these particular symptoms exist. Why are these symptoms appearing in this child's life at this time and in this way?

Can Children Be Mentally Ill?

The simple answer to this question is yes, children can be mentally ill. Serious mental illness, including schizophrenia, bipolar disorder, and other disorders can make their appearance in an individual's life during childhood.

Scientists now believe that major symptoms of a psychosis or serious mental disorder, which almost always features hallucinations and delusions, can emerge during childhood or adolescence as well as during the adult years. Hallucinations, seeing or hearing things that are not seen or heard by other people, and delusions, irrational fixed beliefs, are the two major symptoms of a psychotic disorder. Often, researchers today believe that people are born with their brain hardwired to react with psychotic symptoms. However, it also requires environmental factors, such as extreme or prolonged stress, to release that potential for mental illness. Children could be subject to stresses that might lead to a mental disorder.

FACT

According to the U.S. Surgeon General, childhood mental illness occurs in about 20 percent of children in the United States. However, only about five million children in America have a serious mental illness.

Diagnosing Mental Illness in Kids

Identifying mental illness in children can be a bit tricky. Because of the number of physical, psychological, and emotional changes in children as they go through various stages of development, it is difficult to know what is an expected aspect of development and what is a fairly normal part of childhood, as distinguished from a symptom of a mental disorder.

In order to appropriately diagnose a mental illness in a child, it is necessary and important to take a close look at how a child is functioning in all realms of her life, that is, within the home and family, at school, and with peers. But since preschool children typically only function in one area, at home, a mental health professional does not have the advantage of observing a child in a variety of settings.

There are a number of mental disorders that can affect children and adolescents. These include:

- Anxiety disorders
- Attention-deficit/hyperactivity disorder
- Disruptive behavior disorders
- Pervasive developmental disorder
- Eating disorders
- Learning and communication disorders
- Affective (mood) disorders
- Schizophrenia
- Tic disorders

Schizophrenia in Children and Adolescence

According to some experts in psychiatry and psychology, schizophrenia is both uncommon and difficult to recognize in children. Schizophrenia is a chronic and disabling form of severe mental illness. The exact cause of schizophrenia is not really known. Research today tends to suggest that schizophrenia is caused by a combination of brain changes, biochemical factors, genetic inheritance, and environmental influences.

Although in some regards the symptoms of schizophrenia may be different in children and teens from those in adults, the following symptoms are usually seen in children and adolescents:

- Auditory and visual hallucinations
- Odd and eccentric behaviors
- Unusual and bizarre thoughts and ideas (which may include delusions)
- Confusion of fantasy and reality

- Confused thinking
- Extreme moodiness
- Paranoid thinking
- Severe anxiety and fearfulness
- Difficulty relating to other people, especially peers
- Withdrawn and extreme isolation
- Lack of interest in personal hygiene

Mood Disorders in Children and Teens

When looking at the definition of depression, at least one based on the American Psychiatric Association's *Diagnostic and Statistical Manual of Mental Disorders (DSM-IV)*, depression can be diagnosed when an individual appears to be depressed or has lost interest or pleasure in nearly all activities for at least two weeks. However, depression in children and teens may take the form of irritability and crankiness, rather than the symptoms typically seen in adults of sadness and dejection.

Children and teens who are depressed may withdraw from the family or they may neglect activities they used to enjoy. Depression in young people often interferes with their appetites and eating, and sometimes parents may notice a failure to gain weight.

Major depression in children and teens is characterized by sadness and a loss of pleasure. It is frequently accompanied by cognitive, behavioral, and physical symptoms. Major depression may last between seven and nine months, and once a young person has a major depressive episode, those episodes are likely to recur.

ALERT

Childhood depression is often masked by other kinds of behavioral symptoms. These other kinds of masking symptoms can include hyperactivity, bed wetting, learning problems, and antisocial behavior. Children, especially between the ages of about eight and eleven, do not exhibit depression in the same way adults do. Adults have a slowing of mental and physical activity or display an extreme lack of motivation. Kids may speed up their behavior or act anxious.

Dysthymia

Dysthymia involves a long-standing disturbance of mood. It features ongoing sadness, irritability, and a lack of motivation. Childhood dysthymia lasts an average of four years and about 70 percent of children with dysthymia eventually develop major depression.

Depression and Teenagers

When teenagers are depressed, there is usually an increase in suicidal thoughts, which is quite unusual for younger depressed children. Some researchers see the increase in depression and suicidal behavior at adolescence as being associated with the onset of the changes that go along with puberty. In addition, depression in adolescence may be related to cognitive development and the many stresses and challenges teens must encounter.

As a result, parents may not actually recognize the signs of depression in teens. They may, instead, see changes in their adolescent son or daughter and blame the influence of peers, new friends, or the use of drugs or alcohol. What they may be missing is depression because adolescents don't always show the classic signs of depression that people have come to recognize in adults: withdrawal, sadness and crying, hopeless feelings about the future, and failure to care for themselves physically.

In fact, a depressed teen may still hang out with friends, but they may also become more argumentative or aggressive, they may get into more trouble, or they may start drinking or using drugs.

While trying to deal with all of the pressures of being a teenager, young people between ages ten and eighteen will frequently feel sad, down, or distressed. However, up to 24 percent will have at least one episode of depression that needs treatment during these vulnerable years.

And without counseling or psychotherapy, depressed teenagers are more likely than other teens to abuse drugs and alcohol, fall behind at school, and have behavior problems. Some, of course, are even suicidal.

How Parents Can Help Prevent Depression

Some of the things parents can do to reduce the possibility of depression in adolescents include:

1. Educate children about depression. Children and teens should be given information about depression so they understand the symptoms and know what to do when they feel sad or blue.
2. Help them learn strategies to enable them to cope with difficult situations. Every child is going to be faced with difficult situations, problems, and conflicts. Instead of shielding them from problems or solving the problems for them, teach them how they can solve problems and deal appropriately with conflicts with others.
3. Keep them involved in positive activities. One of the best ways of teaching children to sidestep serious depression is to strongly encourage them to be involved in positive activities and organizations. Not only should they be involved with schoolwork and extracurricular activities, but they should be active with a religious institution, community organizations, charities, and recreational programs.
4. Promote optimism. Research shows that optimists do better academically and socially. Helping a child look on the bright side is a significant life skill to develop. When children think they can succeed, they are more likely to try.
5. Teach them how to manage their stresses. Being overwhelmed by stress often leads to depression. With all the things going on in a teen's life, it might be easy at times to feel completely overwhelmed. Show them how to handle their stresses and what to do to relax when the tension and anxiety builds up.

An Appropriate Psychological Assessment

When a child is suspected of having a psychological disorder or a mental illness, then it is often important to obtain a psychological assessment. A competent psychological assessment consists of psychological tests, interviews, observations, and informal assessment. Information from these various sources must be woven together and made understandable to others.

From this integrated approach to assessment, the psychologist evaluates the strengths and weaknesses of a child in the areas of cognitive and emotional functioning. From this analysis come recommendations for helping the child.

Only a qualified psychologist can conduct a psychological evaluation. A qualified psychologist is one who has a graduate degree in psychology from a recognized university, has been trained in administering psychological tests, and has passed all state and national licensing exams and certifications. In addition, the psychologist should have extensive training and experience in assessing and evaluating a wide assortment of children and adolescents.

What should be in a competent psychological assessment? A competent assessment by a psychologist will usually have the following elements:

- Intelligence testing using a standard individual intelligence test such as the Wechsler Intelligence Scale for Children-Revised
- A brief visual-motor test
- Achievement tests, such as the Wechsler Individual Achievement Test
- Personality testing
- Interview with parents to gather background information, including neurological history, family history, and other relevant data
- Information from the school, including grades and behavior
- Interview with and observation of the child

CHAPTER 14

Children and Stress

All children will be exposed to stress and all children will experience stress at one time or another. Some children will be more vulnerable to stress because of their temperament or because of family problems or other factors. But there are several factors that can help protect children from stress. Being bright, having an easy temperament, being securely attached to his parents, and having the personal resources of those parents help to protect a child. It is important that parents learn to recognize the signs of stress so that they can take action to minimize the effects of stress or do things that are within their power to de-stress their child.

Do Children Experience Stress?

Adults often look at the situations children face as trivial or unimportant. The issues that may cause children to burst into tears or have an emotional meltdown—imagining a monster in their room at night, being rejected on the playground, or getting a low grade in a class—may seem rather insignificant by adult standards. But to a child, these experiences can be devastating.

Child development experts point out that childhood can be a most delicate time of life. It is, in fact, a time during which individuals are perhaps most susceptible to fear, anxieties, and stress. Therefore, childhood stress is real. Whether it is caused by the common problems seen in almost every family, such as sibling rivalry, or whether it is caused by the social problems related to poverty, homelessness, or abuse, stress is very real for a particular child and at times it can be devastating or overwhelming.

Children and Stress

Stress touches all children regardless of culture, gender, age, economic level, or race. The world is not always a child-friendly place and children have experiences that can cause stress at an early age. But children have various experiences just like adults. And just like grownups, particular stressors may or may not adversely affect a child, depending on three factors:

1. How many other stressors the child is already experiencing
2. How much these stressors affect daily life
3. How many protective buffers and coping patterns are in place for the child

In general, a simple, chronic stressor may cause vulnerability in a youngster without really causing any serious or obvious harm. But when one stressor is added to other problems and stresses, even mild ones, a child can suffer considerable damage.

The important question to ask about stress and children is: How much does the stress affect the child's daily life? Some stresses will have little impact on the daily life of a child. Of course, every child will experience some of the numerous possible stressors, those that can be called the hassles of daily living. However, there are ongoing stressful events that will have an impact on the child's life. These stresses, which are far more important than the hassles of daily living, will include poverty, living with an abusive parent, living in a high-risk neighborhood, or living with a parent who is an alcoholic, addicted to drugs, or unable to work or support the family.

Sources of Stress

Sources of stress for children of all ages include:

- Poverty
- Disease
- Homelessness
- Moving or changing schools frequently
- Learning problems
- School failure
- Family fighting and family discord

For school-age children, frequent moving from one home or city to another can be very stressful. Moving and the switching of schools are strongly correlated with low self-esteem, school failure, and parental neglect. Also, for children in the school-age years, poverty is not simply a significant stressor; it can also bring about strong feelings of shame.

Signs and Symptoms of a Stressed-Out Child

Some of the signs of a stressed-out child include depression and sadness, suicidal thoughts, irritability and worsening behavior, decline in schoolwork, and withdrawal. Some child psychologists have suggested that in any child a behavior problem emerges only when there is some accumulation of risks or stresses above the level that the child can handle.

Children experiencing major upheavals, such as their parents' divorce or moving to a new house or new school, show increased behavior problems. These problems may include disobedience, depression, or anxiety. However, an accumulation of stresses is even worse. Michael Rutter, a professor of developmental psychopathology, has found that, in families in which there was only one stress at a time, such as parents arguing or fighting or overcrowding, the children were no more likely to have behavior problems than were children from families with no stresses. But any two stresses occurring together enormously increased the possibility that the child would show serious symptoms.

The particular symptom the child shows in the face of too much stress, whether a behavior problem, withdrawal, depression, or crying, may be determined by the child's temperament, the attachment relationship with the parents, and perhaps even with the discipline used by the parents. But the presence of symptoms may also reflect the excess of stress. In most instances when the level of stress goes down, the child's symptoms disappear as well.

FACT

Children can experience stress at almost any age. For instance, children can be physically or sexually abused at any age and this results in stress. Prolonged stress can lead to feelings such as anxiety, depression, low self-esteem, anger, and hostility. In younger children, stress can show itself in sleep difficulties, loss of appetite, and fearfulness.

Which Children Are Most Vulnerable to Stress?

Psychologists don't have clear answers to this question, but some trends have been observed. For instance, boys seem to be more vulnerable to stress than girls. Also, the child's temperament seems to make a difference. The easy-to-raise child is less likely to have behavior problems resulting from stress than is the difficult child. The child who seems to be able to cope best with stress without lapsing into serious behavior problems is the child who has at least one good, strong, secure relationship with a parent or another adult. Children with secure attachments seem better able to cope with significant life stresses.

Children need stability in order to thrive. They need to know what to expect and they need a predictable world. The degree of stability in a home can determine the amount of anxiety or stress a child might face. If the tone or atmosphere in the home is one of fear or anxiety, if it is chaotic or unpredictable, if it is relatively unstable, then a child may be vulnerable to a higher degree of stress.

Resilience and Coping

For children of all ages, even multiple stresses need not be devastating. Even when kids live in poverty, live with a single, working parent, live with a dysfunctional parent, or live in a high-risk neighborhood, stress of this magnitude need not cause irreparable damage to a child. That is, serious stressors may not be devastating to a youngster if at least one of the parents provides stability and nurturance.

Similarly, children can receive stability from the school and from teachers if those teachers recognize, praise, and encourage their competencies. Also, if a child lives in a community or a neighborhood that cares for its children, there can be important positive effects on kids. Community influences, some researchers have discovered, can counteract the effects of poverty, family discord, and even abuse.

Children are better able to cope with stress if they have one or more of several crucial strengths. The following are critical skills that can sustain reasonably healthy development even in the face of serious problems or significant stressors:

- Good intellectual functioning
- An appealing, social, easygoing disposition
- Self-efficacy, self-confidence, or high self-esteem
- Artistic talents and special abilities
- Academic competence
- Religious faith

In general, children with better developed competence and social skills are able to use coping strategies to deal with their stresses.

The Media and Stress

Television remains the dominant form of youth media. The average American child ages two to six years old will watch one-and-a-half to two hours of TV programming each day. In middle childhood, viewing time increases to an average of three-and-a-half hours a day and then it declines slightly during the adolescent years.

Children who live in lower socioeconomic level families tend to watch more TV than children of higher economic levels, perhaps because there are fewer alternative forms of entertainment available in their neighborhoods or affordable for their parents.

Heavy viewing of entertainment television, in contrast to educational television, detracts from children's school success and social experiences. Yet, more than one-third of children in the United States ages six and younger live in homes where the TV is turned on constantly and about one-third of those children also have a television in their bedrooms.

The Stressful Effects of TV

According to social science researcher David Dutwin, studies have shown that realistic violence, the kind seen in news broadcasts and in documentaries, is far scarier and disturbing than fictional violence. Based on research from the Kaiser Family Foundation, nearly two-thirds of eleven- to sixteen-year-olds watch the news on a typical weeknight. While the percentage of younger children is somewhat lower, still almost two-thirds of elementary school children watch TV news at least sometimes. Dutwin points out that research shows that younger children are frightened by disaster stories and older elementary school children get scared by crime stories.

ALERT

Television and television viewing have been studied extensively since the early 1950s. Obviously, TV can be educational and beneficial to both children and adults. But its negative aspects, such as the amount of aggressive and violent activity it displays daily, have concerned parents and educators. This led the American Academy of Pediatrics to recommend in 1999 that children under two years of age not watch TV, and that older children not have TVs in their bedrooms.

Effects of Television Viewing on Children

Researchers have found that television viewers tend to overestimate the degree of danger and crime in the world and to underestimate the trustworthiness and helpfulness of others. Other studies have shown that the more time eight- to ten-year-olds spend viewing TV, the poorer their reading comprehension.

More recent research has shown that the content of the TV shows children are watching is important. For instance, children who watch child-oriented educational programs between ages two and three do better in reading, math, receptive vocabulary, and school readiness at age five. On the other hand, frequent viewers of general-audience programs performed more poorly on cognitive tests than did those children who viewed less general-audience fare.

Television viewing takes time and may displace other activities, such as sports, reading, or even talking with others. Many TV viewers, it has been found, spend less time with friends, get less sleep, and are less likely to participate in organized sports and other activities outside the home.

Exposure to aggressive models on TV can increase children's subsequent aggressive behavior. Heavy doses of TV violence can affect both attitudes and behaviors, leading children to view violence as an acceptable and effective way to solve interpersonal conflict. But exposure to TV violence affects children differently at different ages due to changes in children's cognitive abilities. Children who can understand the difference between fantasy and reality and between what is acceptable versus what is unacceptable may be affected differently than those children who cannot make these distinctions.

School-Age Children and Stress

During the school-age years children are confronted with challenging and sometimes threatening situations. These kinds of situations require children to try to cope with psychological stress. However, even though children in these middle years may experience stressful life experiences, there is not always resulting psychological disturbance.

Some children are able to overcome the effects of such stresses as school difficulties, family transition, and abuse. Although some school-age kids are relatively resilient and quite capable of handling stress, when negative situations pile up, the likelihood of maladjustment increases as well.

Adolescents and Stress

Most parents might acknowledge that kids today have more pressures and stress. How different is it today as compared to past generations? For one thing, according to some research such as the Child Trends reports, which focus on how American families have been changing, today's youth may be more vulnerable to peer pressure.

According to Nicholas Zill, a nationally known researcher, there are four main reasons why today's young people may have it tougher.

1. Adult authority is weaker and more fragmented.
2. Young people spend more time with peers, and less time with adults.
3. Teenagers have more freedom in their lives than did previous generations of adolescents.
4. The mass media exposes teens to a much broader range of experiences, which may further diminish the influence of parents and other adults.

What is the research that shows the greater influence of peers? Consider these points:

- Studies show that a majority of young people between the ages of ten and twelve want their parents to talk to them more about today's tough issues—issues such as violence, peer pressure, sex, alcohol, and drug abuse.
- Young people usually begin hanging out with gangs at ages twelve and thirteen, and they often join a gang by age thirteen.
- Girls from ages twelve on admit that pressure to have sex comes from boys, girls, their friends, and the media.
- National surveys have found that more than half of sixth graders report peer pressure to drink alcohol.
- One of three sixth graders say they have been pressured to use marijuana.
- Forty percent of sixth graders have felt pressure to smoke cigarettes.
- Nearly half of all teenagers have used illicit drugs before graduating from high school.

ALERT

Today's teens also have to cope with more violence in schools than their parents did. Many teens bring weapons to school—and sometimes use them. Many young people know someone who has died as a result of violence. And many teens know of peers who have overdosed on drugs. Also, there are different pressures on high school students in terms of academics. Teens are taking classes in high school that were previously only taught in college. In order to graduate from some high schools, students often have to pass rigorous state exams.

How Parents Can Help

What does all of this pressure on children and teens mean for parents? For one thing, it means that it is nearly impossible for a parent to truly understand the pressures their children experience, stresses the parent may be unaware of or minimize. But the above research findings related to peer pressures and to the stress related to violence and academic pressure underscore the vitally important role that parents have. It's not just about getting their child involved in sports or extracurricular activities. It's about talking to them about the tough issues.

Since peer pressure can lead kids to make some poor choices, parents must start talking to their kids much earlier than many parents do. Many parents wait until the middle teen years to start talking about peer pressure, drugs, sex, and violence, after some poor choices and decisions have already been made. Since most kids indicate they want their parents to talk to them about the really important issues, it is important that parents start when their children are still in elementary school.

Rather than leading their children to experiment and try out risky behaviors, research shows that when parents start talking about strategies to resist peer pressure early, kids are able to use these strategies when they are needed, and as the research shows, this is as early as ages nine to twelve.

What can parents do to protect children from stress? It is very clear that children of all ages can be helped to deal with stress if they receive social support. The most significant support should come from home. A strong bond with a loving and firm parent can see a child through almost any kind of trauma.

Even in the most difficult situations, say, living in a war-torn region or being homeless, can be tolerable for children if that child has a strong attachment to her parent and that parent has been consistently there and supportive throughout the child's life. In fact, a child growing up with the loving support of a closely attached parent will be resilient and able to deal with many different stressors.

Authoritative parenting, featuring warmth, structure, and high expectations, can provide children a definite advantage. In addition, parents in high socioeconomic levels can also provide advantages to children to help them cope with stress. But besides attachment to parents, children are helped by connections to additional support, which often comes from an extended family. A large family whose members stay connected and offer emotional support to one another can help children weather stress. Personal competencies, family support, and close friends help get most kids through childhood and adolescence without any serious damage.

Stress-Proofing a Child's Life

Parents can help minimize the stress affecting their child. One way to do this is to reduce stress, especially when they recognize that their child already is dealing with one stressful event. For example, if a child is dealing with the separation of her parents, it would be the wrong time to move to a new city or to change schools.

Parents can also make sure that they talk openly about conflicts and issues of concern. Families in which there is an open environment that allows for a sharing of feelings can help reduce anxiety and stress. Likewise, parents can also give their child room to grow. Providing too much structure and setting the expectations too rigidly may feel stifling to a child. Being stifled may add pressure to a child's life. Parents should provide structure and they should provide boundaries, but within those boundaries and within a framework, they can allow children choices and decisions. If parents do not allow children opportunities to make choices as they grow, they may be setting them up for later anxiety and failure.

Parents can also contribute to a stress-free life for their child by giving of their love generously. By showing that their love is unconditional, parents are making it clear that they love their child no matter what. So, even when children misbehave or make mistakes, they can still feel they are loved. In a world in which there is much stress, knowing that a parent's love is always there can be very reassuring.

There are many children who grow up in high-risk families and neighborhoods and surprise everyone by still being successful in life. What is the key?

One study has suggested that nurturing mothering is the real key. When mothers have greater personal resources, they are best able to provide what at-risk kids need in order to cope. By greater personal resources, it means that these mothers have a higher education level, have better mental health, and have had their own nurturing childhood. A child may have several risk factors and may be prone to stress. But if that child's mother can parent that child with several important personal resources, then there's a better chance the child will be stress-proofed.

De-stressing the Stressed-Out Child

A child who is showing obvious signs of stress is in need of help. Think about the child who is sulking, withdrawn, crying more than usual, or screaming in terror at night. These may all be signs of a stressed-out child. But who better to offer some pressure relief than a parent who understands that stress is causing the out-of-the-ordinary behavior?

What helpful measures parents can apply? Consider these:

1. **Use reflective listening.** A child who is stressed out, perhaps because she feels her brother is favored over her or because the teacher has scolded her twice recently, needs to know that somebody is listening to her. That's when a parent can use the mirroring-back technique, or reflective listening. In this approach, you let her know that you understand what she's saying: "It sounds like your brother gets all the attention in this family and no one ever pays attention to you, right?" After she feels she's been heard, the parent may be able to switch gears and talk about solving the problem. But problem solving won't work if a child doesn't think anyone is listening to her concerns.

2. **Take his concerns seriously.** More than just mirroring, sometimes a parent can take a problem seriously in other ways. For instance, if a boy is crying at night because he says there are monsters under his bed, a parent can get involved in the fantasy and do something to "get rid" of the

scary monster. That might mean that an authoritative father commands the monster to leave the room or a powerful mother "chases" the monster out of the room and out of the house with a broom. Parents usually can't talk a child out of a scary belief, but they can take some action that lets the child know that his frightful fantasies are serious business.

3. **Involve the child in decision-making and problem-solving.** Children often feel like they have no say in issues. Things are being done to them, not with them. Parents can change all that by involving them in the decisions that affect them or allowing children to voice their opinions in trying to solve important problems. For example, if a child is anxious because her parents are talking about moving, and she may have to leave behind close friends and switch schools, get her involved so that she has some say in the issue that is likely to have a profound effect on her. If she feels she has had some say in what the family does, she may be more cooperative in living with a decision.

CHAPTER 15

Learning Disabilities

The biggest challenge awaiting children once they navigate the tricky waters of toddlerhood, and learn how to control their emotions and delay their behavioral reactions, is to begin school and start their education. This will be a journey of at least thirteen years, but for many students it will continue past high school and take them through college. But if a child has difficulty learning, the years she spends in elementary school, middle school, and high school could be tremendously frustrating and, indeed, could carry with it an ongoing sense of failure. Learning disabilities hamper the educational experience for many children. For those children with learning problems, the school years are more frustrating than fun.

What Is a Learning Disability?

A **learning disability** is difficulty involving the understanding or use of spoken or written language. This difficulty can appear in listening, thinking, reading, writing, spelling, or mathematics. In order that this difficulty be classified as a learning disability, it must not be primarily the result of visual, hearing, or motor disabilities. Likewise, it must not be the result of mental retardation, emotional disorders, or be related to environmental, cultural, or economic disadvantages.

FACT

According to the National Center for Education Statistics, approximately 14 percent of all children in the United States, ages three to twenty-one, receive special education or related services. The largest category of children receiving special services in public schools is that group of children with learning disabilities. Almost 6 percent of all students are classified as having learning disabilities. In all, 3 percent of all students receive services for speech and language impairment; more than 1 percent are classified as having mental retardation; and almost 1 percent receive services for emotional disturbance.

About three times as many boys as girls are given services for learning disabilities. The explanation for this gender discrepancy, according to some experts, is that boys have a greater biological vulnerability, which makes them subject to greater difficulties of various kinds. On the other hand, some authorities point to a referral bias. That is, boys may be more likely to be referred by teachers for treatment because of troublesome behavior.

The most common learning disability is reading. About 80 percent of children with a learning disability have a reading problem. The three major types of learning disabilities are:

- Dyslexia: A severe inability to read.
- Dysgraphia: A learning disability that involves difficulty in handwriting.
- Dyscalculia: A disability involving difficulty in math computation.

Intelligence and Learning Disabilities

The definition of learning disabilities indicates that in order for a problem to be classified as a learning disability the problem in learning must not be because of visual, hearing, or motor disabilities, nor must it be the result of mental retardation or emotional disorders. In other words, a child must have the potential to learn but is not able to learn under the present circumstances. Therefore, it is important to review the definitions for intelligence, cognition, and mental retardation.

Intelligence and Cognition

Most psychologists agree that intelligence involves the performance of basic mental tasks, which will include perceiving the environment, communicating through language, and performing higher-level tasks such as reasoning, problem-solving, and planning.

Cognition is the mental activity through which individuals acquire and possess knowledge. It includes the functions of perception, learning, memory, reasoning, and thought. A working definition of intelligence may include the idea of cognition. For instance, some experts would define intelligence as: cognition comprising sensory, perceptual, associations, and relational knowledge.

As children grow and develop, there is intellectual development as well. There is a general emergence of intellectual functioning as well as specific patterns of strengths and weaknesses. Because of the specific patterns of strengths and weaknesses, every child will reflect some differences in her intelligence. This pattern of differences is usually quite stable—barring accidents or head injuries—from about ages four or five through adulthood.

There is overwhelming evidence that both heredity and the environment contribute to children's cognitive and intellectual development. From birth, parental stimulation and responsiveness are associated with a child's intellectual functioning. Factors such as parental education, parental interest in academics, and parental beliefs about children's intelligence are associated with higher intellectual levels.

The most frequently mentioned influence from the larger environment is poverty. Children who grow up in poverty may suffer damaging effects in their intellectual development and in their school achievement. The reason for this may be related to factors that go along with poverty, such as inadequate diet, lack of timely access to health services, parental preoccupation with other problems, and insufficient intellectual stimulation and support in the home.

Mental Retardation

Mental retardation involves two types of deficits that are evident before age eighteen:

- Deficits in intellectual functioning
- Deficits in adaptive behavior

Deficits in intellectual functioning means the child is functioning at the lower end of the distribution of IQ scores. IQ stands for intelligence quotient and reflects a measure of intelligence, usually on a **standardized test**. The distribution of IQ scores means that if every person in the United States were given an IQ test and all of the scores were graphed, a majority of individuals would have middle IQ scores, but a smaller percent of people would be high and an equally small percent would be low. Those with mental retardation, or developmental disabilities, would be on the low end of the distribution of scores.

The deficits in adaptive functioning reflect the low end of living in the everyday world. A mentally retarded person's ability to function in terms of cognitive, emotional, and social skills would be lower than most others' abilities.

The American Association of Intellectual and Developmental Disabilities gives this perspective to mental retardation: Mental retardation is a disability characterized by significant limitations both in intellectual functioning and in adaptive behavior as expressed in conceptual, social, and practical skills in day-to-day life.

The term *learning disability* can be used in both a broad and a narrow sense. In the broad sense, it refers to learning problems that can be associated with any type of factor, including mental retardation, brain injury, sensory difficulties, or emotional disorders. But in the narrow sense of the term, learning disabilities refers to the failure on the part of the child who has adequate intelligence and has not been handicapped by his cultural background or by his educational experiences to learn a scholastic or academic skill.

In effect, then, if a child has adequate intelligence, but is not learning a particular skill at a level commensurate with that intelligence, the child can be said to have a specific learning disability.

FACT

The official definition of a learning disability comes from Public Law 94–142, a federal law passed in 1977, in which a specific learning disability is defined as a disorder in the basic psychological processes involved in understanding or in using language, either spoken or written, which may manifest itself in an imperfect ability to listen, think, speak, write, spell, or do math calculations. Unfortunately, not everyone agrees with this definition, and its passage by Congress has brought about controversy in the field of learning disabilities, education, and special education.

Signs of a Learning Disability

Learning disabled children perform poorly on tasks requiring active information processing. When they enter school—these days as early as kindergarten, where they must learn to read, write, and pay attention to instruction given by the teacher—these children are not able to learn as easily or as efficiently as their peers.

ESSENTIAL

What are the mnemonic aids that good students use but learning disabled students do not use? Good readers and good students often come to school with some abilities and skills that allow them to figure out the sound of words or the spelling of words. They may have some initial strategies for doing math problems or for learning to write. Learning disabled students often do not have any of the following aids or strategies: Labeling, verbal rehearsal, clustering, chunking, and selective attention.

Children with learning disabilities do not attend to or remember central information and they have difficulty focusing attention. They often do not have or use rules or strategies to understand, remember, or solve learning problems. They frequently may not have the ability to analyze tasks in ways that will result in the best performance strategies.

They tend to make little use of mnemonic aids such as labeling, verbal rehearsal, clustering, chunking, and selective attention.

- **Labeling:** Labeling refers to making lists or categories of words, ideas, or concepts already learned in order to better understand or learn a new word or idea.
- **Verbal rehearsal:** Verbal rehearsal involves a child's pausing after reading a small amount of a story or selection of text to ask himself—silently or aloud—what he was reading and what it means.
- **Clustering:** Clustering involves grouping known words or ideas together to better enable recall.
- **Chunking:** Chunking involves grouping, finding patterns, and organizing the material a child is trying to learn. Instead of trying to remember or learn every piece of information, if a child can find a pattern, then she can remember the pattern.
- **Selective attention:** Selective attention means paying attention to what seems to be the most important part of a lesson or the instructions.

What Are the Causes of Learning Disabilities?

There is no simple theory or model to explain the cause of learning disabilities. Experts have proposed some of the following theories:

1. Learning disabilities are caused by organic conditions that interfere with learning. These organic conditions include brain injury or brain disease, or other physical abnormalities, such as other diseases or visual diseases or injury.
2. Learning disabilities are caused by immaturity in development.
3. Learning disabilities are caused by other factors such as severe anxiety or depression.
4. Learning disabilities are caused by a failure by the child to acquire the basic academic skills and the reasons would be related to poor teaching

or disruptions in the learning process. Disruptions could be related to inadequate teaching materials, the child's absence from school, excessive absence by the teacher, or the child's moving from school-to-school frequently.

Reading Problems

Approximately 80 percent of children with learning disabilities have a reading disability. Reading disabilities often are referred to by the term **dyslexia**, a word that simply means reading disability. In general, dyslexia refers to a child's failure to master basic procedures involved in reading, such as letter recognition and sound blending.

It is important to distinguish between developmental dyslexia, a failure to develop the ability to read, and acquired dyslexia, a loss of the ability to read after it has already been acquired, such as often comes about as a result of brain injury.

Reading is a highly complex process that involves a variety of cognitive functions. These cognitive functions include attention, concentration, ability to form associations within and between sensory modalities, and such overlapping sub-skills and abilities as phonological awareness (awareness of the sound characteristics of a word), rapid decoding (the ability to recognize words quickly and automatically), verbal comprehension (understanding words and word order), and general intelligence.

Physiological Causes of Dyslexia

Some of the physical or organic causes of dyslexia or other learning disabilities could include:

- Brain damage or brain disease
- Genetic inheritance
- Cerebral dominance (research suggests that good readers have enhanced left hemisphere decoding of written language and reading disability is related to a predominantly right hemisphere–based perceptual coding strategy)
- Ocular factors

Environmental Factors Associated with Dyslexia

Some of the possible environmental factors that may cause dyslexia as well as other learning disabilities include:

- Social class
- Family size
- Childrearing practices by parents
- Family history of reading problems
- School factors
- Level of parental education
- Overcrowding in the home
- Divorce
- Motivational factors in the family and child

Studies seem to clearly indicate that children with reading disabilities frequently have behavioral and emotional problems. These problems include hyperactivity, inattention, and conduct problems. Although behavioral factors may not necessarily cause reading disorders, they may play a role in sustaining reading difficulties.

Who Can Diagnose a Learning Disability?

Either a child or educational psychologist who has the background and experience assessing children with learning disabilities could make a diagnosis. The child or educational psychologist could work in a hospital; in a private psychological, educational, or psychiatric clinic; or as a school psychologist. However, if the psychologist works in a school setting, there are federal guidelines that determine how the finding of a learning disability must be made.

The reauthorized Individuals with Disabilities Education Act (IDEA) was signed into law on December 3, 2004, by President George W. Bush, with the provisions of the act becoming effective on July 1, 2005. The IDEA is a law ensuring services to children with disabilities throughout the nation. IDEA governs how states and public agencies provide early intervention, special education, and related services to the more than six-and-a-half million eligible infants, toddlers, children, and youth with disabilities.

Under this act, a state, along with each individual school district, must adopt criteria for determining whether a child has a specific learning disability as defined in the IDEA. The criteria adopted by any state:

1. Must not require the use of a severe discrepancy between intellectual ability and achievement for determining whether a child has a specific learning disability.
2. Must permit the use of a process based on the child's response to scientific, research-based intervention.
3. May permit the use of other alternative research-based procedures for determining whether a child has a specific learning disability.

Also, under IDEA, the determination of whether a child suspected of having a specific learning disability *is* a child with a disability as defined in the IDEA *must* be made by the child's parents and a team of qualified professionals, which must include:

- The child's regular teacher; or if the child does not have a regular teacher, a regular classroom teacher qualified to teach a child of his or her age.
- At least one person qualified to conduct individual diagnostic examinations of children, such as a school psychologist, speech-language pathologist, or remedial reading teacher.

This group of individuals may determine that a child has a specific learning disability if:

1. The child does not achieve adequately for the child's age or to meet state-approved, grade-level standards in one or more of the following areas:

- Oral expression
- Listening comprehension
- Written expression
- Basic reading skills

- Reading fluency skills
- Reading comprehension
- Mathematics calculation
- Mathematics problem-solving

2. The child does not make sufficient progress to meet age or state-approved, grade-level standards in one or more of the areas that are listed above.
3. The child's insufficient progress is not primarily the result of:

- A visual, hearing, or motor disability
- Mental retardation
- Emotional disturbance
- Cultural factors
- Environmental or economic disadvantage
- Limited English proficiency

To ensure that underachievement in a child suspected of having a specific learning disability is not due to lack of appropriate instruction in reading or math, the group must consider, as part of the evaluation, that prior to, or as a part of, the referral process, the child was provided appropriate instruction in regular education settings, delivered by qualified personnel; and that data-based documentation of repeated assessments of achievement at reasonable intervals, reflecting formal assessment of student progress during instruction, was completed.

Furthermore, the group must ensure that the child has been observed in the child's learning environment (including the regular classroom setting) to document the child's academic performance and behavior in the areas of difficulty. Also, the group must ensure that the child has participated in a process that assesses the child's response to scientific, research-based intervention. Then, each group member must certify in writing whether the report reflects the member's conclusion. If it does not reflect a member's conclusion, that group member must submit a separate statement presenting the member's conclusions.

This process helps to guarantee that parents are involved in the determination of a learning disability and that it is a group decision. Finally, the group must decide if the child is to receive special education services and, if so, what kind of services and how often.

How Is a Determination of a Learning Disability Made?

The assessment of suspected learning disabled children has three major areas:

1. Obtain an estimate of general intelligence in order to determine whether the child has the ability for higher achievement despite past or present performance.
2. Determine areas of impaired functioning that may lend themselves to remediation.
3. Find areas of strength that may prove helpful in remediation efforts.

ESSENTIAL

The indicator most frequently used to identify a learning disability is measuring the ability-achievement discrepancy. Children who are low achievers in school, yet are of average or above intelligence, are eligible for being identified as learning disabled.

Assessment, therefore, is not necessarily an easy or simple task. IDEA, the federal act cited above, says that a school district team may use a discrepancy model that shows that a child is not achieving commensurate with his age and ability levels. If after being given a standard intelligence test and standard achievement testing, a child is found to have a severe discrepancy between achievement and intellectual ability in any of the critical academic areas, then a finding of a learning disability is possible.

The problem centers around how to define a severe discrepancy between ability, measured by an intelligence test, and achievement as shown on a standard test of achievement in school areas. Although this sounds easy enough, there are various methods of defining a "severe discrepancy." IDEA allows states and schools to use whichever discrepancy model they choose, which means that states and individual school districts can decide how they want to measure severe discrepancy. Is it that the child is achieving at half his current grade placement (for instance, a child who is in the sixth grade is achieving at a third grade level)? Or is it so many grades below what would be expected of a child based on his IQ score (a child with an average IQ, who is in the sixth grade, only achieves at a second grade level in reading, for instance)?

Each state and sometimes each district within a state can decide on which model suits it.

Tests Used to Determine a Discrepancy

The most important tool in the assessment of suspected learning disabled children starts with intelligence testing. The most commonly used intelligence test is the Wechsler Intelligence Scale for Children, the fourth edition (WISC-IV). This is a normed test that has validity and reliability and is an individual intelligence test, rather than a group test. It is not dependent on reading, but measures various intellectual tasks by virtue of subtests. It provides an overall IQ score that can be compared to the standard scores of achievement tests.

Also, achievement tests are used to measure reading, spelling, math, and other important areas of academic achievement. For example, a frequently used achievement test is the Wide Range Achievement Test 4, which has four subtests for word reading, spelling, reading comprehension, and math.

There are some school skills, such as written and oral expression skills and listening comprehension abilities, for which there are no well-normed standardized tests. In such instances, information can be obtained through informal assessments. For example, to assess written expression, an analysis of classroom written assignments can be compared with those of a random sample of other children.

How Are Learning Disabilities Handled?

Interventions for children with learning disabilities often focus on improving reading abilities. Research has shown that intensive instruction over a period of time by a competent teacher can help many children. Instructional programs should be designed to help learning-disabled children acquire problem-solving skills, learn new mnemonic aids, and develop good study habits. These strategies should be made part of their repertoire of learning skills through step-by-step instruction and training that can be generalized to various academic skills.

Legislation in the United States mandates that schools place children who require special supports for learning in the least restrictive environment. What this means is that even though children may be classified as learning disabled and even though they may be assigned to special education classes they should be placed in a situation or class as close to normal as possible. That often means that they receive some or all of their support in the regular classroom along with children who are not in special education. This is referred to as inclusive placement. In inclusive classrooms, students with learning disabilities learn alongside typical students in the regular educational setting for part or all of the school day. This practice is designed to prepare them for participation in society and to combat prejudice against individuals with disabilities that leads to social exclusion.

Learning Disabilities and Communication Problems

Most children acquire language and oral expression quite naturally and without formal instruction. Some children, however, experience serious difficulties in their acquisition of language. These children have a language disorder. Since language and oral expression are crucial to both social and educational processes, speech and language disabilities are classified as one of the important learning disabilities that may afflict children.

There are various aspects of oral expression that may go wrong when children are learning to talk and to communicate with others. Some of these areas that may result in communication disability include:

- **Delayed expression of language.** A child may understand and respond to language, but she is not able to express herself as well as other children her age.

- **Limited expressive vocabulary.** The child may not have the ability to name things. She might recognize a truck in a picture, for instance, but cannot come up with the word *truck*.
- **Limited ability to answer who, what, and where questions.** In order to communicate effectively, a child must be able to answer these types of questions. If she cannot, this is a speech and language disability.
- **Delayed speech sound development.** Some children have omissions, substitutions, or distortions of sounds. For instance, a child may substitute the sound "t" for "sh" words. That child may say "tool" when they are trying to say "school." When children have a poor ability to make the sounds of words, this is referred to as articulation errors.

Speech sounds develop at different ages, and some sounds are not fully developed in some children until age seven or eight. For example, "sh" sounds and sounds using the letter "z" are often later sounds to master for many children.

When children have some of these common speech and language problems, they are sometimes designated as learning disabled and referred to a speech and language pathologist or a speech therapist.

Are Learning Disabilities Related to School Failure?

Not only are students identified as having learning disabilities more likely to fail classes or repeat grades, but they are more likely to drop out of school prior to completing high school than are other students. Research has shown that as many as 58 percent of learning disabled students drop out of school early.

There is no single prominent risk factor predicting dropout; however, there are numerous risk factors that, in combination with each other, raise the probability of a student's leaving high school early. These factors include frequent school truancy, poor attitudes about school, lack of parental involvement, a negative school climate, and a lack of community support for schools. Dropouts are most closely associated with high poverty rates, poor school attendance, poor academic performance, being held back a grade, and disengagement from school. It is learning-disabled students who are most likely to experience low grades, being held back a grade, and feeling uninvolved in school.

CHAPTER 16

Autism Spectrum Disorders

Numerous articles in both the popular press and in scientific journals have indicated the rising rates of **autism** in this country. There has been an expansion of the concept of **autism spectrum disorder**, which may be the reason there has been a corresponding rise in the number of people diagnosed with autism in recent years. This rise has led to a controversy as to whether all these individuals being diagnosed indicate that autism is on the rise, or that, with greater awareness of the disorder, more professionals are diagnosing more children with autism. Or is it that many children are improperly diagnosed with autism?

What Is Autism?

The word *autism* means "abandoned in the self." Autism has been called the most severe behavior disorder of childhood. By definition, autism is a neuro-developmental disorder without a clearly defined genetic basis. Children with autism display deficits in three core areas of functioning:

1. Limited ability to engage in nonverbal behavior required for successful social interaction
2. Delayed and stereotyped language
3. Poor ability to engage in make-believe like other children

Children with autism have severe delays in the development of spoken language, which usually means they have marked impairment in the ability to initiate or sustain a conversation with others. In addition, their use of language is often stereotyped and repetitive, and may even feature strange or idiosyncratic language. Furthermore, children with autism have deficits in their ability to engage in varied and spontaneous make-believe play or social imitative play appropriate to the particular child's developmental level.

There are also some behaviors that often go along with the disorder. For instance, children who display repetitive behaviors, can remember lots of facts, or flap their hands may be autistic.

What Is the Prevalence of Autism?

Autism rates increased 57 percent from 2002 to 2006, part of a decades-long surge of cases as doctors and parents became more aware of the disorder. About 1 in every 110 eight-year-olds in the United States had autism spectrum disorder in 2006, according to the Centers for Disease Control and Prevention (CDC). In general, the CDC estimates the current prevalence at about 1 out of 150 children. Three to four times as many boys are diagnosed with autism, but girls with autism have higher rates of mental retardation.

While more cases are being identified as people become aware of the disorder, the CDC indicates a rise in the number of kids affected "cannot be ruled out." Before 2009, autism was considered a rare condition affecting one in two thousand children. Increases in the diagnosis of autism parallel increases in the diagnosis of **Asperger's syndrome** as well as increases of diagnoses of pervasive developmental disorder (PDD).

In this country, rates of autism vary among states. For instance, rates of autism range from a little more than four cases per one thousand children in Florida to twelve cases per one thousand children in Arizona and Missouri.

What Is Autism Spectrum Disorder?

Different people with autism can have very different symptoms. Experts think of autism as a spectrum disorder, which refers to a group of disorders with similar features. Some children may have mild symptoms of autism, while others may have serious symptoms. The autism spectrum disorder category includes:

- Autistic disorder
- Asperger's syndrome
- Pervasive Developmental Disorder Not Otherwise Specified (or atypical autism)

FACT

Pervasive developmental disorder refers to a group of disorders characterized by delays in the development of socialization and communication skills. Symptoms may include problems with using and understanding language; difficulty relating to people, objects, and events; unusual play with toys and other objects; difficulty with changes in routine or familiar surroundings; and repetitive body movements or behavior patterns.

In some cases, psychologists and other health care providers use a broader term, pervasive developmental disorder, to describe autism. This category includes the autism spectrum disorders above, plus childhood disintegrative disorder and Rett syndrome.

Childhood Disintegrative Disorder and Rett Syndrome

Childhood disintegrative disorder is a condition in which children develop normally through ages three or four and then lose previously acquired motor, language, social, and other skills. Like autism, the cause of childhood disintegrative disorder is unknown.

Rett syndrome is a disorder in which there is typically normal development for a period of time, usually for the first six to eighteen months of life. Then various symptoms appear. The symptoms can include:

- Apraxia (a disorder in which a child is unable to perform tasks or movements when asked)
- Breathing problems (problems tend to get worse with stress; breathing is usually normal during sleep and abnormal while awake)
- Excessive saliva and drooling
- Floppy arms and legs
- Intellectual disabilities and learning difficulties (assessing cognitive skills in those with Rett syndrome, however, is difficult because of the speech and hand motion abnormalities)

Rett syndrome occurs almost exclusively in girls and may be mistaken for autism or cerebral palsy.

What Do the Pervasive Developmental Disorders Have in Common?

The impairments the pervasive developmental disorders have in common involve the areas of:

1. Social development
2. Language and communication
3. Restricted, stereotyped, or repetitive behaviors

The impact of these impairments is wide-ranging. Some experts have said that autism is the most severe psychopathology of childhood since it disrupts the very basic aspects of personhood. Yet, individuals with Asperger's syndrome, mild autism, or other PDDs may be able to function in school, go to college, or hold down jobs, although they may have deficits in some of the areas that are common in autism spectrum disorders.

ESSENTIAL

Asperger's syndrome is a relatively mild autism spectrum disorder in which the child has relatively good verbal ability, milder nonverbal language problems, and a restricted range of interests and relationships. Children and teens with Asperger's syndrome often engage in obsessive, repetitive routines, and preoccupations with a particular subject. However, they may be able to achieve good grades in school and even go to college, although they may seem to lack social skills or be restricted emotionally.

What Causes Autism?

Researchers agree that autism stems from abnormal brain functioning, often due to genetic or prenatal environmental causes. According to the National Institutes of Health behavioral-science researcher Catherine Rice, autism may be caused by a combination of genetic and environmental risks. Studies currently in progress are looking at potential causes including exposure to hazardous pollutants and the added risk of parents giving birth at older ages.

Studies have recently shown that from the first year on, children with autism have a larger-than-average brain, perhaps because of massive overproduction of synapses and a lack of synapse pruning. Synapse pruning usually accompanies development of cognitive, language, and communication skills.

Brain imaging studies reveal that autism is associated with reduced activities in areas of the brain (such as the cerebral cortex) known to mediate emotional and social responsiveness, and thinking about mental activities.

Growing evidence also suggests that children diagnosed with autism have a deficit theory of mind. That means that long after they reach the intellectual level of an average four year old, they have great difficulty with false belief. Most autistic children find it hard to attribute mental states to themselves or others. Such words as *believe, think, know, feel,* and *pretend* are rarely part of their vocabulary.

As early as age two, autistic children show deficits in social skills believed to contribute to an understanding of mental life. Compared with other children who have not been identified as autistic, autistic children less often have established joint attention (the ability to focus on the same object or event as another person), engage in social referencing, or imitate adults' behaviors.

QUESTION

Is it possible my child is autistic because he was vaccinated as a baby? This has been one of the popular theories that has emerged in the last several years related to the cause of autism. There is no reliable evidence that shows that autism and vaccinations are related.

Myths about the Causes of Autism

Many myths have developed around the causes of autism. In fact, Leo Kanner, the psychiatrist who first gave a name to the disorder in the 1940s, promulgated the very first myth. Kanner, back then, suggested that the cause of autism was psychological and he attributed the disorder to children who had cold and aloof parents.

Kanner's idea about what caused autism was never backed up by psychological research. However, his views, which were widely disseminated, caused unnecessary guilt and anxiety among the parents of autistic children.

Since then, however, various other myths have arisen. For instance, it has been suggested that poor nutrition, television, or mercury-based preservatives in vaccines cause autism. There is no scientific evidence for these speculations.

However, people who believe these myths have difficulty letting go of them. Although there is considerable controversy about what does cause autism, much still needs to be discovered before scientists know for sure.

Spotting the Symptoms of Autism

As with many diseases and disorders, when the public becomes more aware of the problem, more people make what amounts to a quickie diagnosis. For example, teachers, speech therapists, social workers, and even educational psychologists diagnose autism based on one or two symptoms and may even suggest to parents that their child is autistic. Sometimes such precipitant diagnoses lead to a child's being labeled as autistic and placed in special education classes.

There is no doubt that the concept of autism spectrum disorder has been expanded in recent years and as a consequence there has been an increase in the number of children diagnosed with the disorder. Whether all the children being diagnosed indicate that autism is on the rise or whether more people have a little bit of knowledge leading to misdiagnosis is a continuing controversy.

Having just one impairment, such as engaging in repetitive or stereotyped behaviors, or having difficulties in social interaction, is not sufficient to diagnose autism spectrum disorder. There must also be impairments in several other areas and the diagnosis must be made based on the criteria as given in the American Psychiatric Association's *Diagnostic and Statistical Manual of Mental Disorders-IV, Text Revision (DSM-IV-TR)*.

FACT

The most authoritative and most widely acknowledged diagnostic criteria for autism and the autism spectrum disorders come from the American Psychiatric Association's *Diagnostic and Statistical Manual of Mental Disorders-IV (DSM-IV)*, which was originally published in 1994. The *DSM-IV* states that in order for autism spectrum disorder to be diagnosed reliably, the difficulty must manifest in three main areas: communication, social interaction, and restricted, repetitive, or stereotyped behaviors.

Standardized Criteria for Diagnosing Autism

The American Psychiatric Association's *DSM-IV-TR* provides standardized criteria to help professionals diagnose autism and other pervasive developmental disorders. The criteria for diagnosing autism from the *DSM-IV-TR* are as follows:

- Six or more items from (1), (2), and (3), with at least two from (1), and one each from (2) and (3):

1. Qualitative impairment in social interaction, as manifested by at least two of the following:

    a. Marked impairment in the use of multiple nonverbal behaviors such as eye-to-eye gaze, facial expression, body postures, and gestures to regulate social interaction

    b. Failure to develop peer relationships appropriate to developmental level

    c. A lack of spontaneous seeking to share enjoyment, interests, or achievements with other people (e.g., by a lack of showing, bringing, or pointing out objects of interest)

    d. Lack of social or emotional reciprocity

2. Qualitative impairments in communication as manifested by at least one of the following:

    a. Delay in, or total lack of, the development of spoken language (not accompanied by an attempt to compensate through alternative modes of communication such as gesture or mime)

    b. In individuals with adequate speech, marked impairment in the ability to initiate or sustain a conversation with others

    c. Stereotyped and repetitive use of language or idiosyncratic language

    d. Lack of varied, spontaneous make-believe play or social imitative play appropriate to developmental level

3. Restricted, repetitive, and stereotyped patterns of behavior, interests, and activities, as manifested by at least one of the following:

    a. Encompassing preoccupation with one or more stereotyped and restricted patterns of interest that is abnormal either in intensity or focus

    b. Apparently inflexible adherence to specific, nonfunctional routines or rituals

    c. Stereotyped and repetitive motor manners (e.g., hand or finger flapping, or twisting, or complex whole-body movements)

    d. Persistent preoccupation with parts of objects

- Delays or abnormal functioning in at least one of the following areas, with onset prior to age three: (1) social interaction, (2) language as used in social communication, or (3) symbolic or imaginative play.
- The disturbance is not better accounted for by Rett syndrome or childhood disintegrative disorder.

The Diagnostic Criteria for Diagnosing Asperger's Syndrome

The *DSM-IV-TR* provides the following criteria for diagnosing Asperger's syndrome and distinguishing it from autism:

- Qualitative impairment in social interaction, as manifested by at least two of the following:

  1. Marked impairment in the use of multiple nonverbal behaviors such as eye-to-eye gaze, facial expression, body postures, and gestures to regulate social interaction
  2. Failure to develop peer relationships appropriate to developmental level
  3. A lack of spontaneous seeking to share enjoyment, interests, or achievements with other people (e.g., by a lack of showing, bringing, or pointing out objects of interest to other people)
  4. Lack of social or emotional reciprocity

- Restricted, repetitive, and stereotyped patterns of behavior, interests, and activities, as manifested by at least one of the following:

  1. Encompassing preoccupation with one or more stereotyped and restricted patterns of interest that is abnormal either in intensity or focus
  2. Apparently inflexible adherence to specific, nonfunctional routines or rituals
  3. Stereotyped and repetitive motor mannerisms (e.g., hand or finger flapping or twisting, or complex whole-body movements)
  4. Persistent preoccupation with parts of objects

- The disturbance causes clinically significant impairment in social, occupational, or other important areas of functioning.
- There is no clinically significant general delay in language (e.g., single words used by age two years, communicative phrases used by age three years).
- There is no clinically significant delay in cognitive development or in the development of age-appropriate self-help skills, adaptive behavior (other than in social interaction), and curiosity about the environment in childhood.
- Criteria are not met for another specific pervasive developmental disorder or schizophrenia.

The Diagnostic Criteria for Pervasive Developmental Disorder

The *DSM-IV-TR* provides the following criteria for diagnosing pervasive developmental disorder (not otherwise specified, including atypical autism) and making the distinction between PDD, autism, and Asperger's syndrome:

This category should be used when there is a severe and pervasive impairment in the development of reciprocal social interaction associated with impairment in either verbal or nonverbal communication skills or with the presence of stereotyped behavior, interests, and activities, but the criteria are not met for a specific pervasive developmental disorder, schizophrenia, schizotypal personality disorder, or avoidant personality disorder. For example, this category includes "atypical autism"—presentations that do not meet the criteria for autistic disorder because of late age at onset, atypical symptomatology, or subthreshold symptomatology, or all of these.

FACT

To make diagnosis a bit more complicated, the American Psychiatric Association is working on a revision of the *DSM-IV*, which will be published in 2013 as *DSM-V*. There will be revised criteria for diagnosing autism spectrum disorder with a child having to meet more specific and stringent standards of impairment.

The bottom line here is that parents and teachers, as well as other untrained and unqualified individuals, should not try to make a diagnosis. A mental health professional with demonstrated expertise in diagnosing autism spectrum disorder should be consulted.

Clarifying the Symptoms of Autism

Some autistic children seem not to recognize themselves as independent social beings. Normally, children learn to recognize their mirror images as themselves around age two. But autistic children, even well after age two, do not recognize themselves when looking in a mirror.

In terms of social relationships, autistic children manifest a lack of attachment and empathy in social relations. Most autistic children fail to develop normal friendships, and their peers typically view them as social isolates.

There are always communication difficulties, and most autistic children will almost always have deficits in both nonverbal and verbal communication. Half or more of properly diagnosed autistic children fail to develop meaningful and useful speech. They mostly have very limited and even bizarre means of expressing themselves. An example of this is echolalia, which is a problem identified in autistic children who are not mute. Echolalic youngsters will repeat what is said to them, sometimes over and over. But even when an autistic child develops speech, they often do not use it effectively for social communication. They rarely chat or respond to the verbal comments of other people.

Along with communication deficits, children with autism have difficulty understanding the facial expressions of emotions and they don't understand or make use of common gestures. For example, the gesture meaning to "be quiet" or the gesture to "come here" would not be understood by an autistic child.

Many autistic children fail to learn or master the tasks necessary to function in the world. As a result, they often need constant help with feeding, dressing, toileting, and cleaning. Although their senses function adequately when tested, they behave as if they have sensory deficits. They often spend much of their time engaging in obsessive self-stimulating behaviors, such as repetitively spinning objects, switching lights on and off, or flapping their hands in front of their eyes.

Autism and the Family

Parenting children with autism and Asperger's syndrome is an obviously difficult task. There are a number of major stresses experienced by mothers, fathers, and by siblings of the autistic child.

According to the Autism Society, a child's autism affects every member of the family in different ways. Parents may need to shift their primary focus to helping their child with autism once a diagnosis is made. This change can put stress on the marriage, the other children in the family, as well as on work, finances, and personal relationships and responsibilities.

The Autism Society reports that the economic and emotional burden placed on families when there is an autistic child in the family is incredible. Often parents have to shift much of their resources of time and money toward providing treatment and interventions for their child, to the exclusion of other priorities. The needs of a child with autism place great stresses on all family relationships, especially with siblings. However, parents can help their family by informing their other children about autism and the complications it introduces, understanding the challenges siblings face and helping them cope, and involving members of the extended family to create a network of help and understanding.

Furthermore, the Autism Society suggests that finding time for prayer can help many families handle the challenges of autism while attending a place of worship may provide a safe, inclusive environment for both the child and family.

Autism and Educational Issues

The 1975 Individuals with Disabilities Education Act mandated services for all children with disabilities. This act meant that children with autism, as well as those with other disabilities, would receive services in school. Children declared eligible for special education services receive an Individual

Educational Program in which a written statement is provided that spells out a program that is specifically tailored for the student.

Children with autism benefit from a well-structured classroom, individualized instruction, and smaller group instruction. Behavior modification techniques are sometimes effective in helping autistic children learn. Recent research concludes that when behavior modifications are intensively provided, and used early in the child's life, they are more effective.

Treatment for Autism Disorders

To date autism has been discouragingly difficult to treat. However, the symptoms of autism are treated—both in and out of schools—through speech and behavioral therapies. Some professionals have increasingly used medications, especially those medications designed to reduce serotonin levels. In some cases, doctors have used antipsychotic medicines to help control outbursts and focus attention to enable autistic children to remain in school. However, some medications do not consistently benefit children and are often accompanied by adverse side effects.

Of the treatments tried, operant behavior therapy appears to be the most effective. Operant behavior therapy is a form of behavior therapy in which behavior is carefully monitored and consistently rewarded with such things as tokens and food. Unfortunately, although the changes this form of therapy produces may help the child in some day-to-day functioning, it usually leaves the child still performing well below the normal range. Operant behavior therapy may be helpful in teaching children basic self-help skills, such as eating and dressing; it is not very successful in teaching language skills. Even when some autistic children do learn words through this therapeutic approach, often it seems that they do not learn the meaning of language.

Although behavior therapy may not be the answer to the problems manifested by autistic children, still behavior therapy may help them develop certain skills they wouldn't have otherwise had.

Various advocacy groups for autism, such as Autism Speaks, a nonprofit advocacy group in New York, still believe that the best hope for autistic children is to make sure they have early access to therapy.

CHAPTER 17

Behavior Disorders

When behavior disorders of childhood or adolescence come up for discussion, it generally means that bad behaviors are being talked about. All of the behavior disorders involve breaking the rules or going against what is right or moral. Often, these bad behaviors have to do with failing to obey parents and other authority figures. Behavior disorders can range from the temper tantrums and the rule-violating behaviors of toddlers to the conduct disorders of older teenagers. While the so-called misbehaviors of toddlers may be part of normal development, **conduct disorders** and the delinquent behaviors exhibited by some teenagers are much more serious and may involve the police or the juvenile court.

What Are Behavior Disorders?

Behavior disorders are a group of maladjusted behaviors that are seen in children from early childhood through adolescence. The term *developmental psychopathology* is used to describe the origin, the course, the changes, and the continuities of disordered behavior.

One way of thinking about the behavior disorders in childhood and adolescence is to view these behaviors in terms of the degree to which they reflect the nature of the control children have over their behavior. For example, a group of behavior problems could be viewed as undercontrolled disorders. In this classification of behavior problems, children and teens typically fail to exercise sufficient control over their impulses and their behavior. Examples of undercontrolled behaviors would include noncompliance, disobedience, rule violations, and aggression. These behaviors are the most frequently reported concerns of parents and school staff. A second group of behavior problems could be called the overcontrolled behavior disorders. This set would include anxieties, phobias, and depression.

When Does Aggression Start?

Children begin to show aggression soon after birth. Babies can display anger and aggression if they are not fed on time or if their food supply is taken away. However, in the infancy stage, aggression usually is displayed through howling, crying, and flailing arms and legs.

True aggression, which may be defined as behavior intended to harm another person, doesn't come along until much later. In the meantime, during the toddler stage of development, children can display various sides to their anger and even show aggression. However, aggression by two- and three-year-olds is mostly related to shows of temper when they are told no.

As children mature, two forms of aggression appear. Instrumental aggression is directed at obtaining something desirable, such as a toy another child might possess at the moment. Hostile aggression, or person-oriented aggression, is more specifically intended to hurt a person either for revenge or as a way of establishing dominance.

As children approach the age of two, they begin to worry about ownership rights. Taking toys from another child becomes a more serious matter.

Between ages two and four, temper tantrums, which are not usually aimed at anyone in particular, are the most common form of anger. By age four, though, about one in three outbursts is directed at a particular person who the child believes has done them wrong. Between ages three and four, physical fights over possessions decrease while verbal aggression, involving threats and insults, increase. Also, person-oriented aggression, in which a child attacks and hurts another child, makes its appearance.

FACT

It is common for people to believe that frustration increases aggression. And, in fact, that is often true. However, it is another common belief that catharsis, the occasional or frequent venting of anger, decreases or eliminates anger and aggression. This is not true. Also, some people believe that aggression can be eliminated through punishment. Although aggression may be suppressed under some circumstances, punishment often does not suppress aggression and it can make it worse.

Disobedience and Noncompliance in Early Childhood

Most children have minor emotional and behavior problems at some point in childhood. For instance, it is common for parents of toddlers to be concerned about the misbehavior and temper tantrums that come along around ages two and three. Parents frequently have concerns that they are the only parents in the world who have a toddler who engages in hour-long meltdowns because they were told no. Or parents of toddlers wonder if it is normal for their toddler to be hitting and biting other children. However, these are typical behaviors and they are, in fact, so common that it is not appropriate to call them behavior disorders. They are episodes of disobedience and anger that tend to get resolved as toddlers mature more and reach the ages of three-and-a-half or four years.

Children with more serious problems of disobedience and noncompliance during the toddler and preschool years are either children who have more challenging temperaments or they are children who have difficult issues in their lives that are contributing to their difficult behaviors.

ESSENTIAL

Temperamental traits are frequently associated with greater disobedience and noncompliant behaviors in young children. Some of the temperamental traits that may place young children at risk for behavior problems include: hyperactivity, impulsivity, short attention span, and stubbornness.

There are also factors in the home and within the family that may contribute to behavior problems in young children as well, such as:

- Chaotic environment
- Harsh and punitive environment
- Lack of structure
- Overly lax parenting style

Parenting the Disobedient and Noncompliant Child

In 1998 the American Academy of Pediatrics (AAP) issued the pediatric organization's first guidelines for effective discipline for parents. Among the recommendations of the AAP were:

1. **Use of positive reinforcement strategies to increase desired behaviors.** For instance, providing positive attention to the child by listening carefully and helping him learn to use words to express his feelings, reinforcing desirable behaviors with frequent praise, and modeling orderly, predictable behavior, respectful communication, and collaborative conflict resolution strategies.
2. **Removing reinforcement or applying punishment to reduce or eliminate undesired behaviors.** For example, letting children know clearly what consequences might be expected for misbehavior, providing a strong and immediate consequence when undesirable behavior occurs (time-out or removal of privileges), consistently providing an appropriate

consequence each time a problem behavior occurs, and delivering instruction and correction calmly and with empathy.

By applying these discipline techniques within an atmosphere of a positive, supportive, and loving relationship between the parent and child, most issues of noncompliance and disobedience can be handled with success.

Temper Tantrums in Toddlers

While many parents know that toddlers have temper tantrums, sometimes when those tantrums are too frequent or too prolonged, they begin to worry. Many parents of two- and three-year-olds know that all toddlers have emotional meltdowns, often over the littlest things. And they also know that, frequently, those emotional meltdowns escalate into episodes of kicking, screaming, beating on doors and walls, or throwing or breaking toys and other objects.

Young children who have frequent, prolonged, and persistent angry temper tantrums may in general be more prone to emotional outbursts, which may mean the child is more sensitive, more easily upset, and quicker to get angry.

There's very little parents can do directly about temperamental traits, since these are inborn characteristics. In the long term, though, parents can help their child learn to deal with his tendency to overreact to situations.

One way to have an influence on a young child's behavior is to model patience and calmness. This is exactly what parents of children who have too frequent tantrums want their child to learn. That is, they want them to learn to be patient and calm. At age three, youngsters learn by imitating the important adults in their lives. As parents remain calm while the child is imploding, parents are teaching her to be calm in a stressful situation—even if it doesn't *seem* like she is learning to be more calm and controlled.

In addition, parents should not try to stop a tantrum once it's begun. When adults try to stop a tantrum in progress, they often end up doing other things that aren't very helpful. For example, if they are hugging their daughter when she is in an all-out temper tantrum, the risk is that the parents may reinforce the tantrum while teaching her that the way to get lots of hugs and to get attention is by being emotionally out of control.

Do Children Outgrow Temper Tantrums?

By age five, the temper tantrums associated with two- and three-year-olds are generally a behavior of the past as children now show enough maturity to get ready to enter kindergarten.

However, there are some five-year-olds for whom temper tantrums are just beginning, and when they occur, can result in severe meltdowns. These five-year-olds who are showing temper tantrums at this rather advanced age are generally perplexing to their parents.

The usual stages of development include learning to crawl, learning to use speech and language, becoming independent (which generally involves saying no and being resistant), and having temper tantrums during the toddler years. Those temper tantrums that most parents find so challenging are important because they help children learn to deal with their frustrations, regulate their anger and other emotions, and find out how to cope with not always having their desires met immediately.

ALERT

Parents who have a five-year-old who is going through this stage of delayed tantrums should try to make sure their child has an experienced and patient kindergarten teacher and they should give that teacher some advance warning about what she's going to be facing. By working together with the teacher in the fall, when kindergarten begins, a child who is prone to throwing tantrums can get through this delayed stage with relative ease.

When their impulses for immediate gratification are thwarted, children are forced to learn how to cope with the resulting frustration and anger. In the process of learning how to cope, they figure out that there are better ways to handle all of the little frustrations of life besides having a temper tantrum.

The "perfect" toddler, however, doesn't have these experiences, and while he might be easier to handle for his parents, he misses out on the important advantages that tantrums provide for him. When he becomes older and encounters new and more complex frustrations, he is not well equipped to handle those frustrations.

Aggression in Younger Children

During the toddler years, roughly twelve months to about four years, many parents are surprised at the changes that take place in their child. Every mom and dad has heard of the "terrible twos," but it seems that far too many just don't think it's going to happen to their child.

Parents need to take an active role to teach their toddler how to control her aggression and interact with others without hitting or biting. Here are some steps to help parents become effective teachers of their aggressive child:

1. Parents should spend alone time with their toddler every day where the focus is on playing, reading, and talking to one another.
2. When the child attempts to hit the parent or another person, the parent should stop him (perhaps by holding his wrist) and tell him that there's "No hitting!" Explain that it hurts others when he hits and that the parent doesn't like it.
3. The parent then tells him what is liked: "I really like it when you are kind and gentle to Mommy." Then, holding his hand, the parent should show him and tell him what kind of behavior is desired: "Be kind to me by gently touching my arm. Like this." As the parent demonstrates holding his hand, he should be given praise for doing it (even though the parent is actually doing it with his hand): "That's right. Mommy likes it when you are gentle."
4. When the child is ready, the parent allows him to try it without guiding his hand.
5. He should be reminded before he is with another person what the parent wants him to do: "When Grandma comes over, I want you to be loving and gentle to her just like I showed you."
6. If or when he hits (or acts in any other aggressive manner) toward another person, then right then and there the parent should go through the previously described demonstration and prompting procedure: "Jill doesn't like it when you hit her. Let's try that again. This time I want you to say hi to Jill and tell her that you want to play with her." The first few times the parent should be down on his or her knees with the child and the other person (whom he has been aggressive toward) and the parent may say the words for the child because he may not be willing or able to do this on his own. This modeling on the part of the parent demonstrates how the child is to do it.

Attention-Deficit/Hyperactivity Disorder

Attention-deficit/hyperactivity disorder (ADHD) is a condition of the brain that makes it difficult for children to control their behavior. It is one of the most common chronic conditions of childhood with about 10 percent of children estimated to have the symptoms that characterize ADHD. The hallmark symptoms of the disorder are hyperactivity, inattention, and impulsivity.

While all children have behavior problems at times, children with ADHD have frequent, severe problems that interfere with their ability to live normal lives. They have greater difficulties at home following directions and concentrating on their homework, and they have problem paying attention at school and avoiding impulsive behaviors.

The Causes of ADHD

Research has been ongoing for at least thirty years to try to determine what causes ADHD. While there have been many theories, including preservatives in food, excessive consumption of sugar, inner ear infections, and vitamin deficiencies, none have been scientifically verified.

The most convincing research thus far points to a genetic cause. The research tends to suggest a link with a gene that regulates the action of norepinephrine and dopamine, chemicals manufactured in the brain. The genetic link tends to be reinforced by statistics. If a parent has ADHD there is a 33 percent chance that the child will have the disorder. If both parents have ADHD, the chance of their child having it too increases. For twins, if one twin has ADHD the chances of the second twin having it are between 71 and 90 percent.

Treatment of ADHD

There are many good treatment options available, and the outlook for children who receive treatment for ADHD is encouraging. In fact, recent research findings indicate that most children who are treated in a variety of ways—rather than in just one—show sustained improvement after three years.

In a study funded by the National Institute of Mental Health and reported in the *Journal of the American Academy of Child and Adolescent Psychiatry*, 500 children were followed for several years. This study found that medication along with behavioral treatment resulted in improvement in the symptoms of ADHD.

However, various studies found that children with ADHD, despite improvements because of treatment, still are at increased risk for delinquency and substance abuse than are non-ADHD children and teens. So, although appropriate, prolonged treatment may decrease the risk for serious behavior problems or substance abuse problems, the risk for these disorders is higher than for other children.

Oppositional Defiant Disorder (ODD)

Older children and adolescents who exhibit oppositional defiant disorder are those who persistently defy authority and break the rules. They make it a point—or so it seems to parents and other adults—to go against established rules and the wishes of adults, especially their parents and teachers. In the most severe forms, they may have run-ins with the police or commit minor delinquencies, such as running away, skipping school, physically fighting with peers and parents, or shoplifting.

Although a good many of the adolescents who are referred to juvenile courts may be diagnosed with oppositional defiant disorder, they do not generally get involved in the degree of criminal behavior that young people diagnosed with conduct disorder do. Their principal goal is to upset adults and they go to great lengths to prove themselves right and make adults look stupid or wrong.

The *DSM-IV* defines an oppositional defiant disorder as a disorder in which there is a pattern of negativistic, hostile, and defiant behavior. Children and adolescents who are given this diagnosis commonly are argumentative with their parents or other adults, lose their temper easily, swear, and frequently show their anger, annoyance, and resentment. They get angry easily, without much provocation, and with apparent little regard for the feelings or rights of others.

Early Signs of Oppositional Defiant Disorder

Teenagers with oppositional defiant disorder were frequently fussy, colicky, or difficult-to-soothe infants. During the toddler and preschool years, when a certain degree of oppositional attitude and behavior is considered normal, such behaviors and attitudes became battlegrounds for power struggles between the young child and the parents. These power struggles often center around such issues as eating, toilet training, bedtime, or sleeping, with extreme temper tantrums resulting.

Later in childhood and in the teen years, youngsters with ODD consistently dawdle and procrastinate, may avoid complying with requests or commands, and, in general, continually frustrate their parents. The relationship that develops between ODD teens and their parents is one that features considerable noncompliance, arguing, and a pattern of interaction that contributes to stress and problems at home. Usually, the struggles that first happened in the toddler and preschool years become more exaggerated in the adolescent years with fights over keeping their rooms neat, picking up after themselves, taking baths or grooming appropriately, using obscene language, complying with curfew, doing homework, and attending school. In almost all instances, winning becomes the most important aspect of the struggle for the teen.

ESSENTIAL

It appears that oppositional defiant disorder arises out of a set of family dynamics and childhood characteristics that begin with a child who by temperament is more difficult and fussier than average, and may even be colicky. The child's parents often feel frustrated and as though they are failures. They also tend to perceive their child as unresponsive or bad and they may come to expect that their child will be oppositional or noncompliant. The child, in turn, may become less compliant and more stubborn, refusing to obey rules and commands.

As parents attempt to assert control by insisting on compliance in such areas as eating, toilet training, or sleeping, the young child becomes more resistant by withholding, or refusing to cooperate. However, as the child grows up this way, he becomes increasingly negative, defiant, and noncompliant. Not only does this behavior happen at home, but it occurs in school as well. In their attempts to bring about compliance, parents, teachers, or school officials remind, lecture, berate, punish, and nag the child.

But such adult reactions do not reduce oppositional behavior. Instead, oppositional behaviors on the part of the child become more frequent and more intense.

In their frustration and continued attempts to bring about compliance, adults tend to be inconsistent in discipline, and often the discipline becomes harsher and more punitive. The child's attitude and behavior become more consistently oppositional and he tends to view all adults as punitive and unreasonable—thus his oppositional and defiant behavior is justified.

Conduct Disorder

Children and teens who are classified as having a conduct disorder may show much more serious negative and oppositional behavior. They usually don't think about how their behavior will affect others, and they often deny responsibility for their actions. Instead, they may blame others or find what seems to them to be plausible reasons to justify their own behavior.

FACT

According to the National Institutes of Health, the prevalence of oppositional defiant disorder is estimated to be about 11 percent in boys and about 9 percent in girls. Boys and girls who show symptoms before age eight are referred to as having early onset ODD; it is likely that treatment will last longer and be less successful. Approximately 6 to 16 percent of boys and 2 to 9 percent of girls meet the diagnostic criteria for conduct disorder.

Conduct disorder is a psychiatric syndrome that is basically characterized by a long-standing pattern of violations of rules along with antisocial behavior. As listed in the *DSM-IV*, the symptoms of conduct disorder usually include aggression, frequent lying, running away from home, and destruction of property. The *DSM-IV* lists four types of conduct disorders:

- Aggression or serious threats of harm to people or animals
- Deliberate property damage or destruction (for example, fire setting or vandalism)

- Repeated violation of household or school rules, laws, or both
- Persistent lying to avoid consequences or to obtain tangible goods or privileges

In order for behavior problems to qualify as a conduct disorder, the *DSM-IV* indicates that there must be at least three specific conduct disorder behaviors present for at least six months.

Teens with conduct disorder often engage in many criminal activities. They do not seem to learn from their experiences or from punishment, and may go from the juvenile court to an adult court.

CHAPTER 18

Anxiety Disorders

Fears, worries, and anxieties are a part of every child's life. Anxiety is a normal aspect of childhood development, and it is a normal byproduct of living in a world in which there are dangers. In fact, fears and worries can be healthy. For instance, children should worry if they are lost in a neighborhood they've never been in before. They should be somewhat anxious if they are about to take a final exam at school. And they should have some butterflies in their stomach if they are about to go on stage to sing in the school's musical play. These kinds of anxieties, worries, and fears provide children with important information about the possibilities of harm, danger, failing to live up to expectations, or the need to prepare for success. But normal fears and worries can turn into severe anxieties. Severe and ongoing anxieties can be paralyzing, debilitating, and harmful to the child if they last too long or if they are too severe.

Fears in Childhood

A fear is a sense of anxiety brought about by a specific stimulus. A child believing there is a ghost in her bedroom closet will feel fear. A worry is anxiety brought about by a possible future event. A middle school student about to take a math exam may worry about passing the test.

There are many kinds of fears that children experience. As an infant, most babies at some point show a fear of strangers. Others may show a fear of vacuum cleaners, animals, or loud noises. During the toddler and preschool years, children show fears about separation from a parent, new situations, and ghosts or monsters. As children get older, they exhibit fears related to dangerous or risky situations, rule breaking, or novel social situations.

While fears are normal for all children, gender plays a role in the fears a child may have as girls display more fears than do boys. Some researchers also say that race, ethnicity, religion, and other social factors may play a role.

However, with the increase of their general knowledge about the world and with an increase in the number of experiences they have, children have fewer fears as they get older. For instance, while toddlers and preschoolers may be fearful of monsters in their bedrooms at night, older children know there are no monsters and those types of fears—based on fantasy—tend to disappear.

Worries in Childhood and Adolescence

Worries, as opposed to fears, involve somewhat more vague concerns about possible threats. The three most common worries among children and teens are related to health, school, and personal harm. Surveys show that a majority of kids, perhaps as many as 70 percent, admit to worrying from time to time. However, the types of worries change over the years.

Preschoolers tend to worry about imaginary and supernatural events. Five- and six-year-olds worry about their physical well-being. And eight- to twelve-year-olds worry about their social and behavioral competence and their psychological well-being. Adolescents worry about their relationships with peers, dating, and their personal image.

Different Fears at Different Ages

Here are the most common fears and the ages they usually occur:

- Birth to twelve months: Loss of support; loud noises; unexpected, looming objects; strangers
- Twelve to twenty-four months: Separation from parents; injury; strangers
- Twenty-four to thirty-six months: Separation from parents; animals, especially large dogs; darkness
- Thirty-six months to six years: Separation from parents; animals; darkness; strangers; bodily harm
- Six to ten years: Imaginary beings; snakes; injury; darkness; being alone
- Ten to twelve years: Social evaluations; school failure; thunderstorms; ridicule; injury; death
- Adolescence: Peer rejection; school failure; war and other disasters; family issues; future plans

How Kids Cope with Fears and Worries

Children and teens put various strategies to use when trying to cope with fears and worries. Some of their strategies are effective—others not so. However, in general, kids use three general strategies:

1. **Emotional strategies:** becoming agitated or upset or seeking reassurance from an adult
2. **Cognitive strategies:** thinking of something else or talking with other people
3. **Behavioral strategies:** avoidance, substance use, or asking for help

Some children, no matter what coping skills or strategies they use, are not successful in reducing or eliminating their fears or worries. The fears and worries are so problematic for some children that they develop an anxiety disorder.

What Is an Anxiety Disorder?

Anxiety disorders are internalizing disorders in which there is excessive worry and excessively fearful behavior. The anxiety has gone from being adaptive to being unhealthy in terms of its intensity, duration, and pervasiveness. Anxiety disorders are very common in children and teenagers, and, in fact, they are among the most frequently diagnosed psychological disorders in young people. All of the anxiety disorders are characterized by inhibition and withdrawal, exaggerated and unrealistic fears and worries, overcontrol, and bodily symptoms.

Among the anxiety disorders found in children and adolescents are generalized anxiety disorder, separation anxiety, phobias, panic disorder, obsessive compulsive disorder, and post-traumatic stress disorder.

FACT

Estimates by researchers indicate that somewhere between 3 and 18 percent of children experience one or more of the anxiety disorders. Between 15 and 20 percent of teenagers have an anxiety disorder.

As with fears and worries, anxiety varies with age, with older children experiencing more anxiety. And girls are diagnosed more frequently than boys with an anxiety disorder.

Generalized Anxiety Disorder

Generalized anxiety disorder is characterized by excessive worrying that is not linked to any one event or situation. It tends to cause children to feel significantly distressed over any number of things. These various worries range from the health of family members to tests at school or to future events. This disorder is not defined by what the child is anxious about, but rather by how severe and chronic the anxious feelings are. It is a common disorder among both children and teens.

According to the United States Surgeon General, children with generalized anxiety disorder worry excessively about all types of upcoming events and occurrences. They worry unnecessarily about how they are doing at school or about playing sports, about being on time, and even about natural disasters, such as hurricanes and earthquakes. The worry that these children and teens experience persists even when the individual is not being judged and has always performed well in the past. Because of their generalized anxiety, many of these children will be overly conforming, perfectionist, or unsure of themselves. Young people with generalized anxiety disorder tend to seek approval and often need constant reassurance about themselves and their performance.

Obsessive Compulsive Disorder (OCD)

Obsessive compulsive disorder brings about extreme anxiety and distress in children. This disorder is characterized by recurrent, time-consuming obsessive or compulsive behaviors that cause distress or impairment. The obsessions may be repetitive, intrusive images, thoughts, or impulses. And the compulsive behaviors, such as hand-washing or cleaning rituals, usually are an attempt to displace the child's obsessive thoughts.

QUESTION

My three-year-old keeps doing the same things over and over. Does this mean he has obsessive compulsive disorder?
Healthy toddlers need to repeat things. For example, two- and three-year-olds love to have the same book read to them at bedtime. You may need a change of pace, but they don't. And they may want to hear the same song over and over. And when they are playing, they may have to play with the same toys in the same ways.

Children with obsessive compulsive disorder often have intrusive concerns about germs and contamination. They may engage in repetitive counting behaviors, such as having to count their steps or how often they have done something. Other common characteristics include fear of harming others, death, and sex. They frequently engage in rituals regarding hand washing, checking and rechecking things (like whether they finished their homework), and they may avoid behaviors because of beliefs that those behaviors will cause harm to themselves or others.

There is evidence from twin studies that there may be both genetic and environmental influences causing obsessive compulsive disorder. If one twin has OCD, the other twin is more likely to have OCD if the children are identical twins rather than fraternal twins. Some children develop the disorder after experiencing one particular type of streptococcal infection. The cause of this form of OCD appears to be antibodies directed against the infection mistakenly attacking a region of the brain and setting off an inflammatory reaction.

The ages of onset are difficult to pin down for OCD. Some researchers have indicated that children with early onset may display the symptoms as early as ages five to nine. Other researchers contend that later onset OCD does not begin until after age seventeen. It can appear in children, though, and boys seem to be at higher risk for OCD than girls.

Toddlers Need for Repetition

Why do young children line up all their cars or Legos in exactly the same way? Why do they have to flick the door stop dozens of times? Why do they have to open and close a closet door, dresser drawer, or a cupboard door 500 times? Perhaps for the same reason they have temper tantrums when parents try to change things. When a parent reads a different book, sings a different song, or makes up a new story, they are not following the script and the plan children have learned.

Kids need to see the world as predictable. That predictability makes it easier for them to learn and to be reassured that, in their own rapidly changing worlds, things are still the same. Repeating actions and behaviors over and over again is also a way for a toddler to further develop her motor skills. Among the things she is learning during the toddler stage are such things as walking, climbing stairs, throwing, pedaling a tricycle or small bike, and coordinating eye-hand movements. Just as it is important for adults to practice certain skills, toddlers must do the same. They have to keep climbing the stairs or throwing a ball, in order to try out a new skill as often as possible.

Finally, repetition is a way for a toddler to control her environment while at the same time finding reassurance in things being the same. A toddler has much more control over her environment than she did as an infant. With an increased vocabulary and many more words at her command, she does have an influence over things around her. But, still, she only has limited control over her world.

Doing things the same way is not an obsessive-compulsive behavior; it's simply a youngster wanting to try new things on her own, practice new skills, and maintain a huge helping of sameness in her life.

Separation Anxiety

It is not uncommon for infants and toddlers to experience separation anxiety. However, parents often misunderstand what separation anxiety is and when it usually appears. For example, a baby will cry if she is not in the same room as a parent. Parents see this as clingy behavior and may worry about a child becoming too dependent, but this is usually an early form of separation anxiety.

Infants under the age of six months don't seem to be bothered when a parent leaves or a new caregiver takes over for a while. But sometime after six months of age, children begin to develop a sense of object permanence. This means that they are beginning to understand that things and people exist even when they're no longer there. When they are left by a parent, they know that parent is not there—they just don't know, however, if or when that parent will be coming back.

A parent's leaving, especially during the ages of about ten to eighteen months, triggers off anxiety and uncertainty. Children of this age will do whatever they can to make sure their beloved parent doesn't disappear. Often that means crying or trying to follow the parent. However, by about the age of two children are much more aware that when parents leave them, they will return soon.

Yet, separation anxiety can resurface at any time after the age of two. There can be many situations in which a toddler or preschooler can experience new bouts of separation anxiety. Many toddlers experience a form of separation anxiety when leaving one parent to stay with another or when they are dropped off at a day care center or at a preschool.

Reducing Separation Anxiety

Parents can take various steps to reduce the anxiety or the distress of separation anxiety:

- A parent can make sure they talk about where the child is going before she is taken some place new. Giving a child some advance warning about a transition can help him to begin to adjust to the transition before it takes place.

- Parents can also make sure they allow some extra time so that they don't have to rush through the transition period. While sometimes a quick goodbye is best, some children need a more leisurely goodbye. They may need a parent to be there while they get used to the new environment.

- It can also be important for a parent to tell the child when she is being clingy that the parent knows that she doesn't want her parent to leave. It is likewise helpful to let the child know how long the parent will be away. Even though she may not be able to fully understand how many hours or days it will be until the parent returns, it is important to let her know that she will see her parent again soon.

- A child might need to take a transitional object (such as a favorite toy or stuffed animal) from her house. The transitional object may even be a favorite blanket or something that belongs to a parent, such as a scarf, a sweater, or a photo. When the child misses her parent, she can touch or hold on to the transitional object to remind herself that her parent will be back soon.

Phobic Disorders

Phobic disorders involve the excessive and exaggerated fears of particular objects or situations. For instance, common phobic disorders include intense fears of spiders, being in an elevator, or driving over a bridge. There are three general types of phobias that can affect children and teens:

- **Specific phobias:** This could be an exaggerated fear of animals, blood, or a natural phenomenon, such as a storm involving lightning.
- **Social phobia:** These are fears of being in a social situation and feeling judged or evaluated by others. Social phobias are not just related to

shyness or being inhibited. Shy and timid children may go to a social event and find it very uncomfortable to start a conversation or to play with other children. However, a socially phobic child wouldn't be able to attend the social event at all. In adolescence, socially phobic teens may not be able to raise their hands in class or meet a friend at a restaurant. Typically social phobias start later in childhood or during adolescence.

- **Agoraphobia:** These phobias involve intense anxiety in places where the individual feels insecure, trapped, or not in control. This could occur any time a person leaves his home, shops in a store, or tries being on a ship. Many people with agoraphobia cannot leave their homes and refuse to go to school.

FACT

Between 2 and 9 percent of children have specific phobias. Approximately 15 percent of children referred for an anxiety disorder are diagnosed with a phobia.

Panic Disorders

A panic disorder is a recurrent, unpredictable attack featuring anxiety and sometimes other symptoms such as a pounding heart, sweating, or trembling. Usually, panic attacks are extremely intense and uncomfortable episodes of anxiety. For example, an adolescent may feel his heart beating and start to race when in a department store. Because of fear this could happen again, he refuses to go back to that particular store. Although panic disorders are usually diagnosed in adults, they may be found in teenagers as well, especially in female adolescents. Often, the teen experiencing a panic attack has a persistent concern about it happening again, particularly in the same situation or place where it first occurred. The individual experiencing the panic attack will have a strong fear of losing control, passing out, or having a heart attack.

Post-Traumatic Stress Disorder

Another type of anxiety disorder is post-traumatic stress disorder (PTSD). PTSD involves a severe and ongoing pattern of anxiety following exposure to a traumatic event. In fact, PTSD can only be identified in the context of a person's specific traumatic experience. Although first associated with adults, there is now evidence that children as young as infancy or toddlerhood can show the symptoms of PTSD.

PTSD has been documented in children and adolescents following hurricanes, earthquakes, and other natural disasters. It also been shown to be related to the trauma children experience during a war, but it can be associated with terrorist attacks, car accidents, child abuse, and family violence.

FACT

Recent studies of children and teens who have experienced prolonged and complex interpersonal trauma, recurrent or chronic physical or sexual abuse, for example, have emphasized the idea of complex trauma. Sometimes also referred to as complex developmental trauma, this is a disorder involving both exposure to chronic trauma and a sort of adaptation to ongoing trauma. Usually such complex trauma takes place in the home or in the child's caregiving environment.

PTSD as a Complex Trauma

Some researchers have suggested that between 25 and 66 percent of children have experienced some traumatic history by age sixteen. Children and teens who live in dangerous neighborhoods or who have been exposed to gun violence are most likely to suffer the effects of complex trauma.

PTSD and complex trauma are anxiety disorders that unfold over time. When they unfold, though, they are likely to affect every aspect of a child's adjustment, which means that the child will perhaps experience some functional impairment. Research suggests that complex trauma as PTSD may result not only in ongoing trauma, but in such long-term consequences as depression, delinquency, and substance abuse.

Treatment for Anxiety Disorders

Effective treatment for the wide range of anxiety disorders is currently available. These include psychodynamic therapy and play-oriented approaches for children. However, the treatment of choice for anxiety disorders is cognitive-behavioral therapy (CBT), which research has shown to be effective in the treatment of panic disorders, phobias, social anxiety disorders, and generalized anxiety disorders.

The cognitive part of CBT helps people change the thinking patterns that support their fears, and the behavioral part helps people change the way they react to anxiety-provoking situations. For example, CBT can help people with panic disorder learn that their panic attacks are not really heart attacks and help people with social phobia learn how to overcome the belief that others are always watching and judging them. When individuals are ready to confront their fears, they are shown how to use exposure techniques to desensitize themselves to situations that trigger their anxieties.

ESSENTIAL

Recent research also indicates that Internet-based treatment with various educational and experiential components presented in interactive formats is effective and well-received by both children and their parents.

Children and teens with OCD who fear dirt and germs are encouraged to get their hands dirty and wait increasing amounts of time before washing them. The therapist helps the person cope with the anxiety that waiting produces; after the exercise has been repeated a number of times, the anxiety diminishes. Teens with social phobia may be encouraged to spend time in feared social situations without giving in to the temptation to flee and to make small social blunders and observe how people respond to them. Since the response is usually far less harsh than the person fears, these anxieties are lessened. People with PTSD may be supported through recalling their traumatic event in a safe situation, which helps reduce the fear it produces. CBT therapists also teach deep breathing and other types of exercises to relieve anxiety and encourage relaxation.

Exposure-based behavioral therapy has been used for many years to treat specific phobias. The person gradually encounters the object or situation that is feared, perhaps at first only through pictures or tapes, then later face-to-face. Often the therapist will accompany the person to a feared situation to provide support and guidance.

CBT is undertaken when children and adolescents decide they are ready for it and with their permission and cooperation. To be effective, the therapy must be directed at the individual's specific anxieties and must be tailored to his or her needs. There are no side effects other than the discomfort of temporarily increased anxiety. Cognitive-behavioral therapy is associated with immediate and long-term improvement for anxiety disorders.

Medication can be combined with psychotherapy for specific anxiety disorders, and this is the best treatment approach for many people. The selective serotonin reuptake inhibitors (SSRIs) appear effective in reducing the symptoms of OCD in children and adolescents, although more clinical trials have been done with adults than with children. Additionally, there are significant side effects.

FACT

Systematic desensitization has been used for many years to treat phobias. Systematic desensitization involves teaching an anxious child how to relax and then how to maintain her relaxed state when exposed to the feared object or situation.

Even with advances in the use of psychological medicines to treat various anxiety disorders, it is likely that CBT will continue to play a central role in providing the most effective treatment strategies for helping children and adolescents cope with anxiety.

CHAPTER 19

The Gifted Child

For thousands of years societies have been concerned with identifying and educating gifted children. In the twentieth century, psychologists studied children who scored in the genius range of intelligence. From these studies, a definition of **giftedness** has evolved. It is agreed that high IQ youth are particularly quick at academic work. They have keen memories and an exceptional capacity to solve challenging academic problems. Yet, IQ tests alone and the ability to accomplish high grades in schoolwork do not tell the full story of human mental skills. Recognition of this fact has led to an expanded conception of giftedness in students.

How Is a Gifted Student Identified?

Simply put, a gifted child is one who has superior intelligence, which is further defined by an IQ over 130 on a standard individual intelligence test. However, in recent years the definition of gifted has been broadened to include not only the ability to achieve superior work in academics but also to include superior talent in one or more areas of accomplishment.

A current definition used in public schools is located in the Elementary and Secondary Education Act and describes gifted students as:

The term gifted and talented, when used with respect to students, children, or youth, means students, children, or youth who give evidence of high achievement capability in areas such as intellectual, creative, artistic, or leadership capacity, or in specific academic fields, and who need services or activities not ordinarily provided by the school in order to fully develop those capabilities.

Characteristics of a Gifted Child

Children who are seen as gifted have some or all of the following characteristics:

- They walked or talked before other children their own age.
- They have an early ability to categorize objects.
- They have the ability to use their imagination.
- They have the ability to concentrate, working on tasks longer than other children their own age.
- They have an interest in collecting things.
- They have an early interest in music, art, mechanics, and math.
- They have a good sense of humor.
- They tend to be self-motivating.

Ellen Winner, in her book *Gifted Children: Myths and Realities*, describes three criteria that characterize gifted children in art, music, or academic domains:

1. **Precocity:** Gifted children are precocious.
2. **Marching to their own drummer:** Gifted children live in a qualitatively different way from ordinary youth. They need minimal help, or scaffolding, from adults to learn, and they often make discoveries on their own and solve problems in unique ways.
3. **A passion to master:** Gifted children are driven to understand the area in which they have high ability. They often develop an intense, even obsessive interest and have an ability to focus. They motivate themselves.

Creative and Talented

Creativity is the ability to produce work that is original and appropriate. It involves producing something that others have not thought of but that is useful in some way. A child with a high potential for creativity can also be described as gifted.

FACT

Is giftedness a product of heredity or environment? The best answer is likely both nature and nurture play a role. Researchers have found that individuals with high status in the arts, math, science, and sports, generally report strong family support and years of training and practice. Deliberate practice is an important characteristic of individuals who become experts in a particular area.

There are tests to assess young people's capacity for creative thought and these tests tend to tap divergent thinking. Divergent thinking means to be able to generate multiple and unusual possibilities when faced with a task or a problem. There are a variety of tests of divergent thinking available, including the Torrance Tests of Creative Thinking and Guilford's Alternative Uses Task.

Children usually only demonstrate expertise and creativity in one or a few areas. For this reason, definitions of giftedness have been extended to include talent. Talent is defined as outstanding performance in a specific field. Talent, like creativity and intellectual giftedness, though, must be nurtured. Studies of the backgrounds of talented children and highly accomplished adults often reveals parents who are warm, sensitive, and devoted to developing their child's abilities, and who provide a stimulating home life with models of hard work and high achievement.

Can Giftedness Be Predicted?

One of the best predictors of who will be a gifted child has little to do with the child directly. It has more to do with the parents and the home. What this means is that the best predictor at eighteen months of age as to which child will have high cognitive ability later in the preschool years is to find out what materials are provided to the child and to determine what have been the variety of experiences offered to the child. These research findings illustrate the importance of the quality of the environment provided by the parents in the early stages of the development of a child's giftedness.

The scientists who have studied giftedness are finding that children who are gifted are usually not gifted in many different areas. Rather, research is focusing on domain-specific areas of interest and mastery. Therefore, discovering a particular child's domain-specific talent and then providing that child with appropriate and optimal educational opportunities needs to be accomplished by the time of adolescence in order for that child to be able to take advantage of his own talents and abilities. In other words, many children may be born with the capability of brilliance in a certain area, but the environment and the home life must stimulate and nurture the child's potential.

Parents can play a significant role in helping their children to maximize their intellectual potential. Mothers and fathers can stimulate their child's curiosity, creativity, and intellectual achievement in the following ways:

- By reading to their child
- By providing playmates who will stimulate their child's thinking and be peers with whom she can communicate
- By taking their child to museums, historical sites, concerts, and providing various other cultural opportunities
- By answering their child's questions
- By encouraging fantasy play
- By allowing her to make some of her own decisions

Myth: Gifted Children Have Psychological Problems

It is a long-existing myth that children with superior intelligence are maladjusted individuals. In studies of the gifted conducted by psychologist Lewis Terman, who followed a large sample of gifted individuals for several decades, the gifted were well-adjusted people and many went on to be successful professionals. Despite their autonomy and extensive success in their occupations, as older adults these gifted individuals placed more importance on achieving satisfaction in their family lives, and most thought they had achieved such satisfaction.

Other studies of the gifted have concluded that gifted individuals tend to be more mature then others, have fewer emotional problems than average people, and usually have grown up in a positive family climate.

FACT

The National Association for Gifted Children estimates that there are about three million gifted children in the United States. This represents about 6 percent of all students in this country. However, if the exceptionally talented children are included in this population, then the percent could be somewhat higher.

Determining Whether a Child Is Gifted

A determination of whether a child is gifted is based on the results of individual intelligence testing. A gifted child would score in the superior range of intelligence. This means that on the Wechsler Intelligence Scale for Children-IV (WISC-IV), for example, the superior range would be at the 98th percentile (a child scoring at the 98th percentile would score higher than 98 out of 100 children taking the test) and that would translate into an IQ score of 130 or higher.

While individual and comprehensive intelligence tests, such as the WISC-IV, are valuable in identifying children who are intellectually and academically gifted, they do not offer insight into other areas of giftedness such as artistic ability, creativity, or leadership. In addition, intelligence test results should be interpreted by a professional examiner who is trained in understanding the complexities of giftedness since scores may mask the strengths and weaknesses of children with both gifts and learning disabilities.

Who Should Administer Tests to Determine Giftedness?

Testing for giftedness can be done at school or parents can have it done privately. Many school districts, however, use a group IQ test to screen for gifted programs. These tests can both under- and over-identify gifted children sometimes. The administration of a comprehensive IQ test (usually the WISC-IV or the Stanford-Binet Intelligence Scale-V) offers a more valid and reliable picture of a child's learning needs. No matter where an intelligence test is administered, the testing should be conducted by a qualified and trained psychologist with experience in identifying gifted students.

QUESTION

My three-year-old child seems very bright with a surprisingly large vocabulary. Should I have him tested for a gifted program?
There are IQ tests for children as young as age two; however, testing for giftedness is usually not warranted for children at this age. All pre-school age children, including those that are later identified as intellectually gifted, benefit from enriched environmental, social, and emotional stimulation prior to starting a formal school program. During the preschool years, the child's own emerging interests and abilities should guide parents as to the type of supplementary early stimulation to provide.

Early Testing May Not Be Reliable

As a caution to parents, it is important to keep in mind that early testing may not be reliable. Intelligence test results, particularly in the form of an IQ score, obtained before approximately age four may be highly unstable. Children with exceptional verbal skills will perform better when these intelligence tests are administered during the preschool years. Such scores become much more stable after about age four-and-a-half and continue to stabilize as children get older.

If a parent is seeking to explore school options for a child who appears to be precocious, they might wait until their child is somewhat older than four to get an objective view of their child's learning needs. Of course, it is best for parents to get as much information as possible in order to make informed decisions. The information from testing could be used to decide when to enroll their child in kindergarten, or help determine the need for early enrollment in first grade, or for special school programming. Furthermore, parents may want to consider an accelerated program in one or more subject areas. Some parents may seek testing to help determine if their child qualifies for enrollment in a private school program or an outside enrichment program where their child can explore his interests alongside other very bright peers.

Options for the Education of Gifted Children

Some of the options for educating gifted children include early admission to school, acceleration, special enrichment, special classes, or a special school.

Early admission involves starting a child in school before the traditional age of five or six. A precocious four-year-old might start kindergarten a year or so ahead of the time she would ordinarily have to wait to start school.

By accelerating, a child can skip a grade or attend an ungraded school. For example, a very bright four-year-old with a large vocabulary and the advanced ability to read and write may go directly into a first grade class, thereby bypassing kindergarten. Acceleration is more effective than enrichment when a child's area of expertise is mathematics.

Enrichment is usually provided within the classroom in the form of extra work and special projects. For instance, a teacher could give the intellectually superior student in her class more advanced reading materials or a special essay that he could write on an area of interest.

Gifted children may also benefit from instruction in special classes. Some school districts provide classes for the gifted and talented (usually referred to as GATE classes: Gifted and Talented Education). Teachers in these classes should be experienced and emotionally well-adjusted teachers, who are also intelligent and able to accept the challenges encountered with gifted and talented students.

Teaching Gifted Students

The best approach to teaching gifted and talented youth is for the teacher to engage the student in critical thinking tasks, model responsibility, offer leadership, and provide creative assignments. Gifted students thrive in learning environments that permit them to choose topics for special projects, take intellectual risks, reflect on ideas, and interact with like-minded peers.

Although it is known what tends to work best for teaching gifted students who are intellectually superior and have outstanding academic abilities, in reality it is often the case that the talented students get overlooked and shortchanged. That is, young people who are talented in the visual and performing arts (music, drama, dance, and theater) and in the athletic areas, or students who possess other special aptitudes, tend to get deprived when it comes to special classes and a unique approach to teaching. This is one of the reasons that schools for the arts have been instituted in some school districts.

Public Education Classes for the Gifted

There has been criticism of the education of gifted and talented students in the United States in recent years. Experts say students are being under-challenged and this neglect leads superior students to become disruptive, skip classes, and lose interest in achieving.

Author Ellen Winner and others have stated that it is extremely important for teachers to challenge children who are gifted to reach high expectations. These experts have also observed that, too often, gifted young people are socially isolated and not challenged sufficiently even when in GATE programs. Whenever gifted children are insufficiently challenged they lose their drive to excel. This has led to recommendations that gifted students be allowed to attend advanced classes in their area of exceptional ability. This could even mean that arrangements be made for them to take college classes even though they may still be taking some classes in middle school or high school.

Although many schools offer programs for the gifted, debate about their effectiveness focuses on factors irrelevant to giftedness. These other factors include issues related to whether to provide enrichment in regular classrooms, whether to pull children out for special instruction, or whether to advance brighter students to a higher grade.

Social and Emotional Issues Related to Gifted Children

Gifted students are often viewed by their peers, and sometimes by teachers, as nerds. As a result, they often spend much time alone. However, they may also be socially isolated because their highly driven, nonconforming, and independent styles leave them out of step with their peers. But there is another factor that makes them seem socially isolated. That is that these students often enjoy solitude, which is necessary for them to develop their special talents.

Nonetheless, gifted students still desire gratifying peer relationships and some, more often girls than boys, try to hide their abilities in order to become better liked. Compared with other young people, gifted youth, again, especially girls, report more emotional and social difficulties, including low self-esteem and depression.

ALERT

Some parents and teachers might think that a child who is underachieving in school could not possibly be gifted. But the truth is that gifted students may become bored or frustrated in an unchallenging classroom situation that caused them to lose interest, learn bad study habits, or distrust the school environment.

School Problems of the Gifted and Talented

Gifted students may demonstrate remarkable strengths or talents in some areas, but they may display disabling weaknesses in others. Research from The National Research Center on the Gifted and Talented supports the idea that underachieving gifted students have difficulty actualizing their talents and gifts without differentiated instruction. Underachieving but gifted students tend to fall into a variety of categories:

- Female, especially during adolescence
- Member of a nondominant cultural group
- Student with other identified disabilities, such as a need for learning support, emotional support, or speech and language support
- Student with a physical disability
- Student with significant discrepancies between measured verbal and performance abilities on an intelligence test
- A lower socioeconomic background
- A nontraditional learner
- Student who demonstrates at-risk behaviors

The goals for gifted underachieving students include helping them develop various school survival skills and tactics. In working with these students sometimes an initial task is to teach them self-regulation strategies, including taking time for reflection about their actions. This can be accomplished through individual or group discussion or through informal journal keeping. Further, they need to be helped to try to understand their personal issues of underachievement. That might begin with a discussion of what the label of "gifted" means to them and to others who interact with them.

Teachers of the Underachieving Gifted Students

Experienced and successful teachers of the underachieving gifted need to establish a classroom atmosphere where students will be willing to take risks. This means that the students must feel that on both an academic and a social level they will be treated with dignity and respect and never made to feel different.

Within such a classroom, a gifted support program has to have both intellectual and academic components. For instance, students at the elementary grades may be asked to choose a long-range project in their area of interest, completing it as a practitioner in the field would, and then presenting it to an audience of peers, parents, and other students. To be able to do this, elementary students are first taught the basic skills that practitioners need, which would include research techniques, planning for short- and long-range goals, deciding who the audience will be, and then tailoring the product to the audience. In addition, they would learn how to develop a rubric and timeline with the teacher for the development of organizational and evaluation skills by the student themselves.

Students in middle schools could be offered several themes each year as students continue to individualize their interests through their choice of topic and completion of a project. In addition, in sixth and seventh grades, advanced readers (determined by standardized tests) would participate in literary circles once or twice a week. Often, these groups would include underachievers as well as normally achieving gifted students. At the high school level, students work with gifted support teachers on both intellectual and social or emotional issues. Instead of a project, however, teachers and students might select topics of interest, and these are discussed during the times students are scheduled to participate in the program (traditionally once or twice a week). Teachers may select newspaper or magazine articles, short stories or essays, or a video clip from a television news magazine.

Such programs have been shown to be successful because teachers of the gifted work with classroom teachers as both a resource for materials and as a way for classroom teachers and specialists to understand the individual students more clearly. Also, parents, students, and staff should all be very comfortable with the model of the program, which allows students free rein to explore topics they might not ordinarily be able to pursue. Further, underachieving gifted students are never placed in a class of just underachievers or just high achievers. All students are allowed in all classes and there is no "gifted track" where only identified gifted students may participate.

The idea of this kind of programming (of gifted support) is to help all gifted kids reach their potential, and to affirm their special gifts, despite individual behaviors and differences that might stand in their way.

Raising a Gifted and Talented Child

Parenting a gifted child can be joyful and can make parents proud. But it can also be challenging. Parents can influence the development of intellectual superiority, creativity, and talent. But there are a few things parents of the gifted should keep in mind:

- Don't place undue burdens on your child just because she is gifted.
- Focus on the positive aspects of your child's behavior.
- Allow time for unstructured play and activities.
- Provide structure and limits as you would for any child.
- Continue to provide an environment that is enriched with lots of materials and opportunities for exploration.
- Allow your child to make choices and some of his own decisions.
- Help him learn to balance his life so he doesn't suffer from stress and burnout.
- Help her establish outlets for her creativity

CHAPTER 20

Getting Help

There are many things parents can do to influence and help their children and teens. But there are times when parents have exhausted their resources and conclude that it is time to seek professional help. However, some parents may not be sure if professional assistance is necessary. Or if they are sure, they do not know how to proceed. What kind of help is needed? Where do you find it? What do you ask a therapist? How do you tell your child about getting help? These are all-important questions that need to be addressed. Getting the answers facilitates getting the right kind of professional help a child or adolescent requires.

Recognizing When Professional Help Is Required

It isn't always easy to tell when outside help is needed, nor is it easy to tell if a serious problem exists. Of course, most parents would agree that, if a teenager tries to commit suicide, it is definitely time for professional assistance. Or if a child is so out of control that he is destroying the house and disrupting the family, most would agree that it's time to call on the services of a child psychologist. But there are many other situations when it is not quite clear if there is a serious enough problem. Maybe it is something the child will outgrow or perhaps it is just a temporary problem that will go away on its own.

However, there are some ways to determine when a child or adolescent requires outside help. Here are some indicators that professional help is needed:

- He is persistently withdrawn.
- She is engaging in self-destructive behavior, such as suicide attempts, use of dangerous drugs, cutting and self-mutilation, or excessive dieting.
- He is exhibiting recent and drastic changes in personality.
- There is a marked and unexplained deterioration in school performance.
- He is showing compulsive behavior that interferes with daily life.
- She has fears and anxieties that are incapacitating.
- There are repeated outbursts of violent or sadistic behavior.
- He is out of touch with reality.

In addition to these signs of serious problems, parents should also be aware of these other signs of a serious problem that requires professional help:

1. The problem has gone on continually for six months or longer.
2. Efforts within the family to try to change things have been unsuccessful.
3. The child or teen cannot bring about changes despite repeated assurances that he will try.

Parents may want to help their child cope with problems, but there are some behaviors and symptoms that are beyond the scope of what parents or family members can do to help. These include:

- A severely depressed mood
- Hyperactive and unfocused activity
- Destructive and violent behavior in the home
- Repeated delinquent and criminal behavior
- Repeated and prolonged alcohol abuse, including binge drinking
- Use of dangerous drugs over a period of time
- Severe dieting and significant weight loss
- Suicidal gestures and attempts
- Hallucinations and delusions

If a child or adolescent shows any of these symptoms, parents should not delay getting professional help.

Dating Abuse

There are other situations that frequently concern parents that might require counseling or professional help. One such example is dating abuse and date violence. The Centers for Disease Control and Prevention have called teen dating abuse a serious problem in the United States. Research suggests that at least one in four adolescents experiences verbal, physical, emotional, or sexual abuse during dates each year. Nearly one out of every ten high school students says she has been physically hurt by someone she was dating.

ALERT

Dating abuse and intimate partner violence has a negative and often long-lasting effect on individuals. Teenagers who are abused are more likely to do poorly in school. They may engage in unhealthy behaviors like drug and alcohol use. Not infrequently, abused teens carry the patterns of violence into future relationships. Research indicates that abused teens are three times more likely than their nonabused peers to experience violence during college.

Dating abuse can include shoving and hitting, but can also take the form of yelling, name-calling, manipulation, and possessiveness. Often an adolescent who is abusive can make the person he is dating feel guilty if she tries to break up with him. And when parents try to intervene, they often are shut out as the teen begins to be more secretive about what's really going on in the relationship. The reason for this secrecy is that the teen doesn't want to be told she should break off the relationship. Furthermore, adolescents in an abusive relationship are embarrassed or ashamed about the abuse they're experiencing, or they are convinced it is their fault they are being abused.

Encopresis

When parents find there is no medical or physical reason for a child of four or older to have bowel movements in his clothes during the day, there is usually a need for professional consultation. Generally, most children establish bowel control before they gain control of their bladder. Usually by age three, most children are potty trained—at least to some degree—and then have a decreasing number of accidents. However, when children are beyond this age and they have previously shown themselves capable of being completely potty trained, but still have accidents, something else is going on. There is a name for such bowel movement accidents: encopresis.

A child is said to be encopretic when she is physically normal but regularly soils her pants. Encopresis is the persistent defecation in underpants or in private places, such as corners or closets. Most often, encopresis stems from emotional problems or behavior problems. Some encopretic children are diagnosed with oppositional defiant disorder. The emotional problems that may give rise to encopresis may relate to significant and ongoing stress or from parent-child relationship problems.

Helping the encopretic child is not a matter of applying discipline. Being angry or shaming the child will not cure the problem. In fact, such approaches may make it worse. Therefore, the assistance of a child or family therapist is required. Together with a therapist who is skilled in handling such problems, the parents and therapist together can begin to examine the battles or conflicts within the family and analyze the parent-child relationship. It is well for parents to keep in mind that children with encopresis need immediate professional attention. To delay can lead to other problems, such as self-image problems. Children who are encopretic are usually easy targets for ridicule and derision by others at school or in play groups.

Running Away from Home

Estimates are that every year more than one million teenagers run away from home. The National Runaway Switchboard reports that 86 percent of runaways are between the ages of fourteen and seventeen, with 74 percent female and 26 percent male.

Often parents don't know exactly what to do if their child has run away. Most states have no mandatory reporting laws when a child or teen runs away, so parents typically are not obligated to file a report with the police. In the 1990s, however, federal legislation was passed directing police departments to take reports immediately on any missing children under age eighteen, including runaways. Under the law, that information must be entered into the National Crime Information Center, a computerized database of victims and criminals maintained by the FBI. However, that doesn't mean the police will start to search immediately. In fact, most police departments don't. And many police departments fail to report runaways to the National Crime Information Center.

Although it may be traumatic for parents when a child or adolescent runs away, it can be an important indicator that there are family problems that must be addressed. While a parent's reaction to a child's return may be a combination of relief and anger, the real work then begins to try to figure out why the child left home and how to prevent this behavior from happening again. This work requires parents to listen and for the child and parent to communicate to try to solve whatever problems led the child to leave. If this type of communication is not possible, the family should seek professional help from a counselor or therapist.

Before Taking Your Child to a Therapist or Counselor

If a child is a worrier, does she need professional help? What if he has sleep problems? What about a child who seems to have obsessive-compulsive traits? Or a teenager who repeatedly talks back to her parents? One such problem may not be a good reason for rushing a child off to a therapist. Having a particular problem does not necessarily mean that she is in need of psychological help. Before taking a child or adolescent to a counselor or therapist, parents may need to look at the other side of the picture. What are her strengths? Where is she doing well? Are the one or two problems interfering with day-to-day life? Is the problem debilitating? And how does the child feel about the problem? Is she accepting of the way she is? Does she see the problem as something that needs to be fixed?

If a child is not too upset by the problem, or if it is not interfering with a significant part of her life, professional help may not be needed. On the other hand, if it is an ongoing issue, if it has defied all efforts to bring about change, and if it does interfere with a child's day-to-day life, at least a professional consultation might be the next, logical step.

Getting an Evaluation

There are many concerns that parents may have about their child. Some of those concerns may be aspects of normal development. Others may be bizarre or strange; or they might be very annoying or disruptive to the family. So, what should parents do?

A first step could be a referral to a child or adolescent psychologist for a psychological evaluation or a psychological assessment. By having an experienced child psychologist conduct an assessment, some or all of a parent's questions could be answered. The psychologist would provide a report, which would include a diagnostic statement and recommendations for what needs to be done to help the child or adolescent cope better.

What Is a Psychological Assessment?

When a parent doesn't know what is really bothering his child or when he is not sure if a serious problem exists, the next step may be to obtain a comprehensive psychological evaluation. Such an evaluation or assessment consists of a battery of tests, a personal interview with the child, an interview with the parents, or information obtained from other resources, such as the school and medical records.

In addition to standardized tests, such as an intelligence test and personality inventories, psychologists usually do a clinical interview with the child and the parents. The purpose of these interviews is to learn more about the child's perceptions of the problem and to learn more about the youngster's emotions. Furthermore, the interview with the youth will help the psychologist gain a general impression of the youngster's appearance, language capabilities, and social skills. The psychologist will also want to establish rapport so that if the same psychologist ends up doing therapy with the child a relationship has already been established. The interview with the parents is very important in learning more about the child's history and development, and more about family dynamics. A psychological evaluation may take three hours or longer and may cost several hundred dollars.

Finding a Therapist

There are several types of helping professionals trained to work with children and adolescents. Helping professionals can include psychologists, psychiatrists, social workers, and counselors. The best way to find a therapist is to consult with your child's pediatrician, the family doctor, or a school counselor. Family members and friends can also be excellent resources for a good recommendation. Also, professional organizations, such as the state psychological association, can be an excellent place to obtain a list of professionals in the area and their specialties.

It is important in selecting a therapist for a child that the professional be an expert in the particular problem area manifested by your child. For example, not every therapist who treats children or teens is an expert in such specialty areas as attention-deficit/hyperactivity disorder, eating disorders, or suicidal behaviors.

Qualifications of Therapists

Any therapist or counselor you are considering should have appropriate credentials. Generally, this means that the professional must have the following:

- A degree from an accredited graduate program
- Completion of a professional licensure program
- Completion of supervised clinical experience
- Qualification for a state's license or certification in their field

This would mean, for instance, that a psychologist should have a master of arts (MA) or a doctorate (PhD), be licensed by the state (say, as a licensed psychologist), and have completed supervised training in areas relevant to the child's problem. Similar qualifications would be required for a psychiatrist, a social worker, or a counselor.

What to Ask a Therapist

In order to try to select a therapist or clinician who might be best suited to your child or adolescent, it is best to ask some questions first. Among the questions you should ask before scheduling an appointment are:

1. What is your background?
2. Are you licensed?
3. Have you worked before with the kind of problem the child has?
4. If so, what has been your success?
5. What approach would you use in treating this child?
6. How long do you think it would take to treat this kind of problem successfully?
7. Will you provide feedback to the parents about your general progress?
8. What kind of medical insurance do you accept and what would be the co-pay? Or, if the insurance runs out (or the parent has no insurance to cover psychological treatment), what are your fees for a session?

Having obtained answers to these questions, the parents will be better equipped to decide which therapist they would like to have work with their child.

Types of Treatment

There are a variety of types of treatment offered by professionals in the mental health field. Listed below are the major types of professional help you are most likely to encounter in seeking a professional for a child or adolescent:

- **Psychotherapy:** One of the most common approaches to treating children and adolescents is talk therapy. Often simply referred to as outpatient therapy, the clinician may take an eclectic approach to treatment. That is, the therapist may combine various forms of treatment, but the focus will be on developing a relationship with the child and engaging in one-on-one treatment to work on goals selected by the therapist and child together.
- **Cognitive-Behavioral Therapy (CBT):** Cognitive-behavior therapy focuses both on the child's thoughts as well as their behavior. The idea is to help the individual change any misperceptions or inaccurate or distorted thoughts while also developing better coping behaviors. CBT approaches usually help young people develop more effective social skills and help them practice those skills.
- **Psychodynamic Therapy:** This form of therapy focuses on past experiences to help children and teens achieve insight into how their emotional or psychological problems developed. Early childhood experiences are examined and these are put into the context of current problems as individuals learn to manage their emotions and behaviors more effectively.
- **Group Therapy:** Many different kinds of therapy can be provided in a group setting. Children and teens may be able to be more open about their problems and their behaviors when in a group with their peers. In addition, other group members can provide helpful feedback to others in the group and this feedback may be more acceptable coming from a peer than from the therapist who is the group leader.
- **Family Therapy:** Family therapy is based on the idea that a family is a system and that if there are changes in one part of the system the rest of the system may change as well. Another important aspect of family therapy is that if a child has symptoms of emotional or behavioral problems, the family therapist will treat it as a family problem rather than as the child who needs to be fixed. This helps children and teens more readily accept and make use of treatment.

- **Play Therapy:** Play therapy involves the therapeutic powers of play to help children resolve psychological problems. Generally, play therapy is used with very young children or nonverbal children.

Talking to Your Child about Therapy

While younger children may not be given any advance warning that they are going to be talking to a therapist, both younger children and teenagers need a certain amount of preparation before attending a first therapy session.

Young children need a simple explanation as to why they are going to talk to a stranger. For instance, a young child can be told that, "We are going to be going to see a talking doctor today. She is going to help you with the problems you've been having with other children at school."

Because teenagers often have a sense of the stigma (at least in their perception) of seeing a therapist, they usually resist seeing a therapist to talk about problems. Often they see having to go to a "shrink" as evidence that someone (for example, their parents) think they are crazy. Therefore, this misperception has to be addressed in telling them about therapy. A parent could say to a young teen: "Because of the depression and sadness you've been feeling lately, I've scheduled an appointment with a therapist today. This is not because I think you are crazy or have a mental illness, but it's because I love you and am worried that we haven't been able to help you feel better."

Older adolescents can be resistant about therapy as well. They may feel they are being treated as a child or that they are being told what to do. While parents can attempt an explanation, it may fall on deaf ears if the teen hasn't previously admitted there is a problem. It's sometimes better if the appointment is with a family therapist to reduce the feeling they are being singled out or blamed for the family's problems: "We are all going to see a therapist tomorrow to try to solve some of the problems we have with communication in this family."

In general, giving children and teens advance warning and an explanation about going to see a therapist helps to prevent resistance.

Teenagers, Behavior Disorders, and Family Therapy

When adolescents present serious behavior problems at home or at school, often parents try various ways to deal with the problem. The things they try could include therapy, counseling, hospitalization, or medication. However, individual therapy is usually not the answer for teens with behavior problems. They often don't respond well to one-on-one sessions because they can deny problems, shift the blame to other family members, or lie to the therapist. However, a skilled family therapist might be more productive because some of the conflicts and communication problems within the family can be addressed. Group therapy, when available, could also be useful in improving the social skills adolescents with behavior problems often lack.

Hospitalization Might Be an Option

In some instances it is best to hospitalize a child or teen with serious problems, particularly a problem that may require medication. Hospitalization can sometimes serve as a time-out both for the family and the child, especially if there has been considerable stress and tension. While hospitalized, the staff can find the right medication for the youth and get the medicine stabilized before he returns home. Hospitalization may be the first treatment of choice in situations where the child is threatening suicide, has been violent toward others in the family, or is in danger of overdosing on drugs or alcohol.

Boot Camps

Sending a child or adolescent to a boarding school or a military school may be the best answer for some young people. However, these schools can send the wrong message sometimes. For instance, not only is there a strong message that the child is the problem and needs to go away in order to be cured, but sending a child away suggests that the family will function much better with the child living somewhere else. One of the other drawbacks to a boarding school or a military school is that while the child or adolescent may make a positive adjustment while living away from home, when he returns home and begins to live in the previous environment with the same family dynamics, his behavior may deteriorate.

Boot camps get a great deal of positive publicity in the media, but there is a lack of evidence that a militaristic approach benefits adolescents with behavior problems. While it makes some sense that adolescents would learn positive behaviors in a rigid, structured program, research indicates that troubled teens who are sent to boot camps either do not improve or get worse.

Correctional boot camps were designed with the idea of combining a get-tough approach with education, substance abuse treatment, and social skills training. But research shows that boot camps are ineffective in reducing the acting-out behavior of teens with behavior problems. Furthermore, some states have closed down their boot camps because of abuse of kids.

ALERT

Like boot camps, scared-straight programs or modified scared-straight programs for adolescents often get favorable media attention. However, ever since the first scared-straight program, which was presented and filmed in Rahway State Prison in New Jersey, researchers have been studying these types of programs. There is *no* evidence that they are effective with teens with behavior problems. If anything, they tend to make kids more likely to engage in delinquent and criminal behavior.

Juvenile Courts

In some cases the best answer for a teen with a serious behavior problem might be a juvenile court. Many acting-out teens need the firm rules, consequences, and structure a juvenile court can provide. In addition, juvenile courts often have a range of auxiliary services: parent training classes, group therapy, and probation services.

There are disadvantages to a child or adolescent coming under the jurisdiction of a juvenile court. The parents lose control of what services the child will receive and will not be able to decide when the child will be released from court jurisdiction. However, many out-of-control or behaviorally disordered teens need the controls a court can provide.

Medication as a Treatment Approach

Various medications have been used to treat anxiety, obsessive compulsive disorder, ADHD, serious mental illness, and various other disorders and symptoms in children and teenagers. All of the psychotropic medications are designed to affect the neurotransmitters (the brain chemicals) in the brain. While some of these medications, such as those typically used to treat ADHD, have been designed for this purpose, still it is important to remember that most medications used by psychiatrists have been tested on adults and not on children.

QUESTION

My daughter is a very anxious twelve-year-old. Would she benefit from medication?
There are medications, such as Catapres or Clonidine, which are used by physicians to treat anxiety and hypertension. However, many psychotropic medications used by psychiatrists and other physicians have not been sufficiently tested on children or teens. Thus, they pose a risk when used with children.

All medications have side effects and the potential side effects need to be considered before agreeing to allow a child to be treated with medication. In general, more children and adolescents are being treated with psychiatric medications than at any other time in history. Yet, there are some facts to keep in mind about medications. First, the antipsychotic medications tend to work very well in controlling the symptoms, such as hallucinations and delusions, of serious mental illnesses. Second, medications are generally not effective in reducing defiance, opposition, behavior disorders, or substance abuse. Third, it is difficult to control the use of medication by children and teens, particularly if they have to take a dose of medication during the day when they are at school.

Finally, in almost all instances in which medication might be helpful for a child or teen, the use of medication should be viewed as only one component of treatment. Usually, medication should be seen as an adjunct to other forms of therapy or counseling.

APPENDIX A

Questions and Answers

How can I help my child gain self-control?

When young children are out of control, it's often helpful to remain calm and patient. It is important in dealing with children that you always keep the long-range goal in mind. In most instances the long-term goal is to help them avoid getting out of control in the future and help them regain control more quickly in the future. Take a patient approach because that will represent strength to your child. By remaining calm yourself, you are sending a message to your child that you are not frightened or upset by her loss of control and that will help your child feel less afraid and anxious.

What can I do to ease separation anxiety?

Don't hurry or pressure your child. Instead remain patient while reassuring him that you will return. In most instances, it is best not to prolong your goodbye. Make sure your goodbyes are matter-of-fact and brief. Long goodbyes suggest you are anxious about separation and that simply indicates to your child that there is a reason to be upset about parting from you.

How can I help my child deal with stress?

Talk openly with your child about the stress. Help her to talk about what's bothering her and encourage her to express her feelings. Tell her that many children her age and older would be pressured by the same situation, but reassure her that she—or that you and she together—can take steps to reduce the stress. Ask her what she thinks she could do to handle her anxiety and help her decide on some strategies that she can implement. Support the strategies she wants to use and tell her that after she tries them the two of you should talk again to see how they worked out.

What can we do to help our child make friends?

A child of any age may not know or be able to list the specific actions he can take to increase friendships. However, the first thing to do is to find out if he is concerned about friends and his relationships with peers. Just because a child seems to be isolated doesn't mean that he feels isolated or friendless. But if he expresses feelings of loneliness or rejection, then ask him to make a list of things he can do to make and keep friends. There are several strategies that work well for most children in making friends. These include talking to other people every day, addressing them by name, asking questions about their interests, and doing kind things for them. Help your child get in the habit doing these things every day and he will likely make several new friends.

How can I help my child overcome shyness?

It is very important to avoid reinforcing or encouraging shyness and timidity. Don't tell her she is shy and don't let her hear you describe her as shy when you are talking about her to others. Instead, let her know that you expect her to be outgoing and to interact with others. Although interacting with others may be difficult for her, let her know that you have confidence in her doing those things that are difficult. In other words, don't make excuses for her and don't allow her to act in a shy manner. That only makes matters worse. Encourage her to face situations that cause her anxiety and praise her efforts to overcome her inhibitions.

How can I improve my child's self-confidence?

The first thing you can do is to make sure you are not doing anything to hurt his self-confidence. That means that you never belittle him, treat him as incompetent, or discourage him from expressing his opinion or trying things on his own. On the other hand, use praise and attention when he makes choices, puts forth efforts to do the difficult, and shows courage to try new things. When praising him, tell him specifically what you liked about what he did. For example, you could say, "I'm very proud of you for raising your hand in class to ask a question about the problem you didn't understand. That took courage and you should feel good about yourself for doing that."

Why does self-esteem drop during adolescence?

Self-esteem often dips during the teenage years, especially for girls, because the adolescent years are a time of physical and emotional change. As teens are changing, they are not sure how these changes are affecting them and how their peers are reacting to the way they are changing. Times of transition are always difficult for people and most of adolescence is a time of transition. In addition, teens are trying to figure out who they are and they are not sure who exactly they should be and whether others will accept who they are. As they become more sure of who and what they are and where they fit, they begin to feel better about themselves. Parents can help the process of teens' gaining self-esteem by giving praise and compliments and avoiding criticism and derogatory remarks.

Glossary

Adolescence:
The developmental stage that leads from childhood to adulthood, and which starts at about ten years of age and ends at around twenty years of age.

Aggression:
Behavior that intentionally harms other people by inflicting pain or injury.

Amygdala:
That part of the brain that controls emotions.

Apgar score:
A widely used method to assess the health of newborns at one and five minutes after birth.

Asperger's syndrome:
A relatively mild autism spectrum disorder in which the child has fairly good verbal skills but has a restricted range of interests and relationships.

Attachment:
In child psychology it refers to the close bond that develops between an infant and the primary caregiver.

Attention-deficit/hyperactivity disorder (ADHD):
A childhood disorder characterized by inattention, impulsivity, and hyperactivity.

Autism spectrum disorders:
A range of disorders that include autism, Asperger's syndrome, and what may be called pervasive developmental disorders. All of these disorders are characterized by problems in social interactions, verbal and nonverbal communication, and repetitive behaviors.

Autism:
A severe developmental disorder featuring early onset and deficiencies in communication and social interaction.

Child development:
The study of the pattern of movement or change in children's social, cognitive, and emotional capacities that begins at conception and continues throughout childhood and adolescence.

Cliques:
Small groups of children that range from two to twelve individuals in which children share similar interests.

Cognition:
The mental activity through which children acquire and process information.

Conduct disorder:
A behavioral disorder in which a child or adolescent violates rules and society's norms, and in which the individual has little regard for the rights or property of others.

Continuity-discontinuity issues:
A question in developmental psychology about whether development in children involves gradual, cumulative change (continuity) or distinct stages (discontinuity).

Corpus callosum:
The area of the brain where fibers connect the brain's left and right hemispheres.

Difficult child:
A temperamental style in which a child tends to react negatively and cry frequently, engages in irregular routines, and is slow to accept new experiences.

Down syndrome:
A form of mental retardation that is transmitted through chromosome irregularity.

Dyslexia:
A type of learning disability involving a severe impairment in reading ability.

Easy child:
A temperamental style in which a child generally reacts in a positive way, establishes regular routines, and adapts easily to new situations.

Embryonic period:
The period of prenatal development that occurs two to eight weeks after conception.

Fetal alcohol disorder:
A cluster of abnormalities and problems that is seen in babies and children born of mothers who drink alcohol during pregnancy.

Fetal period:
The period in prenatal development that lasts from two months after conception until birth.

Gender:
The characteristics of children as males and females.

Gender identity:
The sense of being male or female that is acquired by most children by about age three.

Gender role:
A set of expectations that directs how boys and girls are to think, act, and feel.

Germinal period:
The stage of prenatal development that takes place in the first two weeks after conception.

Giftedness:
The possession by a child of superior intelligence or superior talent or creativity.

Hormones:
Chemical substances secreted by the endocrine glands and carried through the body by the bloodstream.

Identity:
A child or adolescent's sense of who they are.

Infancy:
The stage of development that lasts from birth to about twelve months of age.

Insecure attachment:
A type of attachment shown by babies who have not formed a stable bond that allows them to explore their environment.

Intelligence:
The ability to learn or understand.

Intelligence quotient (IQ):
A score derived from an intelligence test that allows comparisons with the way others his or her age have performed on the same test.

Learning disabilities:
Disabilities involving understanding or using spoken or written language and which interfere with learning in school.

Low birth weight:
Babies that weigh less than five-and-a-half pounds at birth.

Mental retardation:
A condition of limited mental ability in which the individual has a low IQ, usually below an IQ of 70, and which interferes with an ability to adapt to everyday life.

Myelination:
The process of encasing axons in the brain with a myelin sheath that increases the speed of processing information.

Object permanence:
Piaget's term for the ability of an infant to understand that objects and events continue to exist even when they can no longer be seen or heard.

Peers:
Individuals who share the same age or maturity level.

Phenylketonuria (PKU):
A genetic disorder in which a child cannot properly metabolize an amino acid, and which, if left untreated, results in mental retardation and hyperactivity.

Piaget's theory:
A theory that states that children actively construct their understanding of the world and go through four stages of cognitive development.

Prefrontal cortex:
A part of the brain involved in reasoning, decision making, and self-control.

Prenatal period:
The period of child development that lasts from conception to birth.

Scaffolding:
Adjusting the level of parental guidance and support to fit the child's efforts and helping the child to be more skillful.

Securely attached infants:
Babies who have a solid bond to their parent or caregiver and use this bond as a secure base from which to explore the environment.

Self-esteem:
The overall evaluation of the self; also called self-worth or self-image.

Slow-to-warm-up:
A child whose temperament is characterized by inactivity and mild, low-key reactions to environmental stimuli. This is a child who adjusts slowly to new experiences.

Standardized test:
A test with uniform procedures for administration and scoring. It allows for one child's performance to be compared to another child's performance.

Stranger anxiety:
An infant's fear of and wariness toward strangers; it tends to appear between six and twelve months of age.

Temperament:
Refers to the individual's typical mode of response to the environment. It accounts for differences that children have in their responses to people and situations.

APPENDIX C

Resources

Recommended Readings

American Psychiatric Association. *Diagnostic and Statistical Manual of Mental Disorders*, IV—TR (4th ed.). Arlington, VA: American Psychiatric Publishing, 2000.

Boesky, L. *When to Worry: How to Tell If Your Teen Needs Help and What to Do About it.* New York: American Management Association, 2007.

Byron, T. *Your Toddler: Month by Month.* New York: DK Publishing, 1998.

Califano, Joseph. *How to Raise a Drug-Free Kid: The Straight Dope for Parents.* New York: Fireside, 2009.

Curtis, G.B. and Schuler, J. *Your Baby's First Year: Week by Week.* New York: Da Capo, 2005.

Klass, P. and Costello, E. *Quirky Kids: Understanding and Helping Your Child Who Doesn't Fit In; When to Worry and When Not to Worry.* New York: Ballantine Books, 2003.

O'Shea, K. and Windell, J. *The Fatherstyle Advantage: Surefire Techniques Every Parent Can Use to Raise Confident and Caring Kids.* New York: Stewart, Tabori & Chang, 2006.

Sears, W. and Sears, M. *The Successful Child: What Parents Can Do to Help Children Turn Out Well.* New York: Little Brown, 2002.

Shelov, S.P. & Hannemann, R.E. *Caring for Your Baby and Young Child: Birth to Age 5.* New York: Bantam Books, 1998.

Steinberg, L. & Levine, A. *You and Your Adolescent: A Parent's Guide for Ages 10–20.* New York: Harper Perennial, 1991.

Winner, Ellen. *Gifted Children: Myths and Realities.* New York: BasicBooks, 1996.

Websites

American Academy of Pediatrics
www.aap.org

American Academy of Family Physicians
www.aafp.org

American Psychological Association
www.apa.org

Autism Society
www.autism-society.org

For information about ADHD and other childhood disorders and problems
www.nimh.nih.gov/health/publicationsattention-deficit-hyperactivity-disorder

Selected Developmental Milestones in a Child's Life

Although all children are different and unique, these are milestones that many children reach by the ages indicated below:

Three Months of Age

Motor Skills

- Lift head when held at your shoulder
- Lift head and chest when lying on his stomach
- Turn head from side to side when lying on his stomach
- Follow a moving object or person with his eyes
- Often hold hands open or loosely fisted
- Grasp rattle when given to her
- Wiggle and kick with arms and legs

Sensory and Thinking Skills

- Turn head toward bright colors and lights
- Turn toward the sound of a human voice
- Recognize bottle or breast
- Respond to your shaking a rattle or bell

Language and Social Skills

- Make cooing, gurgling sounds
- Smile when smiled at
- Communicate hunger, fear, discomfort (through crying or facial expression)
- Usually quiet down at the sound of a soothing voice or when held
- Anticipate being lifted
- React to "peek-a-boo" games

Six Months of Age

Motor Skills

- Hold head steady when sitting with your help
- Reach for and grasp objects
- Play with his toes
- Help hold the bottle during feeding
- Explore by mouthing and banging objects
- Move toys from one hand to another
- Shake a rattle
- Pull up to a sitting position on her own if you grasp her hands
- Sit with only a little support
- Sit in a high chair
- Roll over
- Bounce when held in a standing position

Sensory and Thinking Skills

- Open his mouth for the spoon
- Imitate familiar actions you perform

Language and Social Skills

- Babble, making almost singsong sounds
- Know familiar faces
- Laugh and squeal with delight
- Scream if annoyed
- Smile at herself in a mirror

Twelve Months of Age

Motor Skills

- Drink from a cup with help
- Feed herself finger foods like raisins or crackers
- Grasp small objects by using her thumb and index or forefinger
- Use his first finger to poke or point
- Put small blocks in and take them out of a container
- Knock two blocks together
- Sit well without support
- Crawl on hands and knees
- Pull himself to stand or take steps holding on to furniture
- Stand alone momentarily
- Walk with one hand held
- Cooperate with dressing by offering a foot or an arm

Sensory and Thinking Skills

- Copy sounds and actions you make
- Respond to music with body motion
- Try to accomplish simple goals (seeing and then crawling to a toy)
- Look for an object she watched fall out of sight (such as a spoon that falls under the table)

Language and Social Skills

- Babble, but it sometimes sounds like talking
- Say his first word
- Recognize family members' names
- Try to "talk" with you
- Respond to another's distress by showing distress or crying
- Show affection to familiar adults
- Show mild to severe anxiety at separation from parent
- Show apprehension about strangers

- Raise her arms when she wants to be picked up
- Understand simple commands

Eighteen Months of Age

Motor Skills

- Likes to pull, push, and dump things
- Pull off hat, socks, and mittens
- Turn pages in a book
- Stack two blocks
- Carry a stuffed animal or doll
- Scribble with crayons
- Walk without help
- Run stiffly, with eyes on the ground

Sensory and Thinking Skills

- Identify an object in a picture book
- Laugh at silly actions (as in wearing a bowl as a hat)
- Look for objects that are out of sight
- Put a round lid on a round pot
- Follow simple one-step directions
- Solve problems by trial and error

Language and Social Skills

- Say eight to ten words you can understand
- Look at a person who is talking to him
- Ask specifically for her mother or father
- Use "hi," "bye," and "please," with reminders
- Protest when frustrated
- Ask for something by pointing or by using one word

- Direct another's attention to an object or action
- Become anxious when separated from parent(s)
- Seek attention
- Bring toys to share with parent
- Act out a familiar activity in play (as in pretending to take a bath)
- Play alone on the floor with toys
- Compete with other children for toys
- Recognize herself in the mirror or in pictures
- Seem selfish at times

Two Years of Age

Motor Skills

- Drink from a straw
- Feed himself with a spoon
- Help in washing hands
- Put arms in sleeves with help
- Build a tower of three to four blocks
- Toss or roll a large ball
- Open cabinets, drawers, boxes
- Operate a mechanical toy
- Bend over to pick up a toy and not fall
- Walk up steps with help
- Take steps backward

Sensory and Thinking Skills

- Like to take things apart
- Explore surroundings
- Point to five to six parts of a doll when asked

Language and Social Skills

- Have a vocabulary of several hundred words
- Use two- to three-word sentences
- Say names of toys
- Ask for information about an object (asks, "shoe?" while pointing to shoe box)
- Hum or try to sing
- Listen to short rhymes
- Like to imitate parents
- Sometimes get angry and have temper tantrums
- Act shy around strangers
- Comfort a distressed friend or parent
- Take turns in play with other children
- Treat a doll or stuffed animal as though it were alive
- Apply pretend action to others (as in pretending to feed a doll)
- Show awareness of parental approval or disapproval for her actions
- Refer to self by name and use "me" and "mine"
- Verbalize his desires and feelings ("I want cookie")
- Laugh at silly labeling of objects and events (as in calling a nose an ear)
- Enjoy looking at one book over and over
- Point to eyes, ears, or nose when you ask

Three Years of Age

Motor Skills

- Feed himself (with some spilling)
- Open doors
- Hold a glass in one hand
- Hold a crayon well
- Wash and dry hands by himself
- Fold paper, if shown how
- Build a tower of many blocks

- Throw a ball overhead
- Try to catch a large ball
- Put on shoes (but not tie laces)
- Dress herself with help
- Use the toilet with some help
- Walk up steps, alternating feet
- Walk on tiptoes if shown how
- Walk in a straight line
- Kick a ball forward
- Jump with both feet
- Pedal a tricycle

Sensory and Thinking Skills

- Recognize sounds in the environment
- Pay attention for about three minutes
- Remember what happened yesterday
- Know what is food and what is not food
- Know some numbers (but not always in the right order)
- Know where things usually belong
- Understand what "1" is
- Understand "now," "soon," and "later"
- Substitute one object for another in pretend play (as in pretending a block is a car)
- Laugh at silly ideas (like milking a dog)
- Look through a book alone
- Match circles and squares
- Match an object to a picture of that object
- Match objects that have same function (as in putting a cup and plate together)
- Count two to three objects
- Avoid some dangers, like a hot stove or a moving car
- Follow simple one-step commands

Language and Social Skills

- Use three- to five-word sentences
- Ask short questions
- Use plurals (dogs, cars, hats)
- Name at least ten familiar objects
- Repeat simple rhymes
- Name at least one color correctly
- Imitate housework or help with simple tasks
- Ask to use the toilet almost every time
- Enjoy being read to
- Talk about feelings and mental states (e.g., remembering)
- Demonstrate some shame when caught in a wrongdoing
- Try to make others laugh
- Play spontaneously with two or three children in a group
- Assign roles in pretend social play ("You be mommy;" "I be daddy")
- Know her first and last name
- Understand "I," "you," "he," and "she"
- Believe everything centers around him ("if I hide my eyes, no one will see me")
- Answer whether she is a boy or girl

Index

We Have

EVERYTHING®

on Anything!

With more than 19 million copies sold, the Everything® series has become one of America's favorite resources for solving problems, learning new skills, and organizing lives. Our brand is not only recognizable—it's also welcomed.

The series is a hand-in-hand partner for people who are ready to tackle new subjects—like you!

For more information on the Everything® series, please visit *www.adamsmedia.com*

The Everything® list spans a wide range of subjects, with more than 500 titles covering 25 different categories:

Business	History	Reference
Careers	Home Improvement	Religion
Children's Storybooks	Everything Kids	Self-Help
Computers	Languages	Sports & Fitness
Cooking	Music	Travel
Crafts and Hobbies	New Age	Wedding
Education/Schools	Parenting	Writing
Games and Puzzles	Personal Finance	
Health	Pets	